STIFLEl

"Insightful and thought-provoking! James dives into all the little things we do to undermine the productivity of our organizations and the people we manage. The business world is moving too fast to not adapt and change with it - if you're feeling behind the curve with your workforce, read this book and take its advice!"

Marshall Goldsmith | New York Times #1 bestselling author of *Triggers, Mojo,* and *What Got You Here Won't Get You There*

I have known Jim for nearly 25 years. His broad experiences throughout his career come out loud and strong in this work as well as what is so desperately needed for future managers and leaders.

Ken Jennings PhD | Best selling co-author of *The Serving Leader* and *The Greater Goal*

James Wetrich has written a counter-intuitive book: most business books try to tell us what we should be doing; this book shows us what we should STOP doing. And there is much that falls under that heading and James Wetrich covers it all, using his long and storied career as a leader to underscore his philosophy. Read it and reap!

Lance Secretan, PhD, | Best selling Author of *The Bellwether Effect* and 21 other books

"If you want to know what it takes to be an effective leader, read this book. Jim Wetrich provides inspirational, practical, and coherent guidance on what works. You will find yourself going back to this book again and again to help determine a path forward."

Richard Chow | Founder and Investor

This is one of the most meaningful books about leadership I have read in the last 25 years of my senior executive career. Jim provides us with a comprehensive leadership and management toolbox to help people and companies sustain their competitive advantage. Jim reemphasizes how and why properly led and developed human capital is our greatest asset to create corporations which are built to last. A must read!!!

Pierre Guyot | Chairman of the board, Limflow SA

James's book is not just an ordinary book about dealing with complex manahement issues, it is survival guide for all employee levels in Corporate America.

I was particularly drawn to the chapter on micromanagement, and his words "You will have people with a lot to say and those that don't like to speak at all. But the volume of the words coming out of a person's mouth shouldn't be an indicator of the value of what they have to offer. Truer words were never said!" I would also add "you can't please all of the people all of the time so don't try."

Bravo James for an exceptional guide to leadership.

CB Bowman, CMC, MCEC, BCC | CEO, Trusted Advisor CEO Association of Corporate Executive Coaches CEO Workplace Equity & Equality www.cbbowman.com

"Jim Wetrich has captured the essence of the issues faced by leadership in today's tumultuous world—including all of those which have come about most recently—as from the pandemic, the millennial generation, the diversity movement, inexcusably poor leaders. He has discussed them in depth and provides solutions for leaders. This is a must read for anyone trying to build an organization and to be successful in leading it. A powerful read for us all."

James G. Ellis | Former Dean, Marshall School of Business University of Southern California

Stifled: Where Good Leaders Go Wrong is an absolute masterclass of leadership books! This book is a real-life blueprint of all things leadership. Jim's decades of work experience, his never-ending desire to learn, and his remarkable gift to teach make this book must-read. I have a bookshelf full of other business books, but this is my favorite! Thanks, Jim!

W. Hays Waldrop | Founder and President, Institute of Healthcare Executives and Suppliers, LLC

"There are some leadership lessons that can only be learned by living. In this book, Jim Wetrich has bottled decades of experience to deliver a crash course in business and life. Reading Stifled is like having an executive mentor in your back pocket."

Tiffany Dufu | Founder & CEO, The Cru

Jim Wetrich delivers on the promise of the title. This book isolates and discusses all the biggest stifles in any organization and then discusses what we can do about them. The book provides a much needed pandemic look at organizational leadership. The last 18 months have challenged leaders in unimaginable ways. The disruption, fear, loss, and loneliness has changed each one of us in ways that we could not have imagined. Coupled with political disruption, racism and pervasive lack of trust, it has been difficult to stay grounded to the principles of leadership that serve as our compass in leading companies.

Big Red provides wisdom and reflection on workplace disruption, the value of work relationships including the destructive element of incivility and our need to focus and strive for real diversity in the places we work. He wisely reminds us that expecting Covid -19 health and safety practices from our employees is not a form of bullying.

While the entire book is quick, insightful reading, certain chapters were like a post pandemic tonic. In addition to the important pandemic lens, he reminds us of the factors that stifle leadership such as needing to be aware of our own inherent biases and how to avoid the toxic element of leadership hypocrisy. The book has the courage to say what we all know that design by committee rarely works and inclusivity does not mean giving everyone a say-so that results in no one having ultimate responsibility and accountability. It's time to revolt again annual performance reviews dictated by archaic human resource practices. All new leaders should read and heed the chapter on leadership transitions.

In summary, Big Red is bringing us back during this pandemic time to the principles that should guide our leadership everyday while also pointing out the critical need to discard old practices that stifle our leadership and frustrate our teams every day.

Linda McCauley | Dean, Nell Hodgson Woodruff School of Nursing Emory University

Leadership and business books pack shelves year after year, but I always seem to struggle with most for two reasons. One, they are not written by leaders, academics. . .yes, researchers. . .yes, but not from those who have been in the trenches, grinding it out year after year and meeting with success. The second is that they are ethereal, inaccessible and don't translate into actionable concepts. Stifled is written by a tried and true leader who took the time to understand the art form, and master it to the letter.

This book is written by a leader. Insightful, accessible and full of wisdom. It reads like a playbook that looks forward more than backwards. If you take the field of battle in a leadership role, this book should be your manual!

Leader, servant, student, teacher, no better friend, no worse enemy, that is "Big Red." This is a leader worth following, and his book is your guide.

Commander Rorke T. Denver USN (Ret.) |
Navy SEAL, NY Times Best Selling author of *Damn Few: Making the Modern SEAL Warrior*

In his book, Jim points out that "there is no standardized assessment or competency process for managers and leaders." This book is a wonderful starting point to educate and mentor today and tomorrow's leaders and managers.

Hector A. Quintanilla, PhD, CPA | Provost and Vice President, of Academic Affairs Texas Wesleyan University

This book is absolutely superb! A well organized and highly relevant compilation of world-class knowledge, experience and wisdom! The breath, depth and relevancy of Critical Leadership Lessons is just amazing! If you are serious about growing, learning, improving and achieving, this book will prove to be a priceless treasure for you!

Read it. . . don't skim it. Study it carefully. . . not superficially. Most important. . . apply this incredible knowledge and wisdom. Application it will significantly change and improve your work, your personal and professional relationships and your life!

Dan Nielsen | Founder/CEO/Publisher, America's Healthcare Leaders

Jim Wetrich has constantly inspired me since we met at Mölnlycke Healthcare. When I started reading his book, I immediately ordered several copies for leaders who will appreciate his experiential roadmap for new & tenured leaders to implement with ease. I recommend "Stifled: Where Good Leaders Go Wrong". You will gain numerous ideas to implement immediately with exceptional results. Jim's quick wit and depth in strategy and political savviness make this book a quick read. "Stifled" provides great insights that illustrate the stupid things that undermine the productivity of organizations and the people we manage. You will be inspired to fix organization challenges and skilled to identify and resolve them. His examples come alive and provide more insights than you can count. Big Red's approach to genuinely connecting with others is evident immediately and is a game changer. Jim's leadership expertise is evident on each page of this book. Jim is a life-long learner who genuinely cares about others and in truly invests in their success.

Big Red has inspired my leadership philosophy; when I met my new learning team, I shared a copy of his personal credo which I keep on my desk to ensure they know what to expect. I strive to emulate Jim's ability to eliminate organizational disfunction and typical challenges in corporations. His leadership messages are timely and current as employee engagement has plummeted during the covid-19 pandemic.

Karen E. Stewart | Associate Chief Learning Officer, Medical University of South Carolina

A candid and personal telling of what's ailing our organizations and most importantly, what we can do about it.

Rick Orford | Co-Founder & Executive Producer at Travel Addicts Life, and bestselling author of *The Financially Independent Millennial*

After this pandemic, we have a golden opportunity to implement some real change. I hope this book is embraced as the guide to do that. I found myself nodding in agreement throughout the entire book. You nailed it.

Paul Gunn | CEO, KUOG Corporation

Perfect for the executive just starting out or the high-level leader looking for a better way forward. No matter who you are, or what stage you are at, you will benefit from this book.

David Fuess | CEO, High Tech

Stifled presents the solutions to some of the gravest problems facing our businesses moving forward.

Orad Elkayam | Founder, Mogi Group

Very well written and full of great approaches to business. I particularly loved the chapter on meetings, as I am sure so many will. It is also timely for the world we live in now.

Mark Nureddine | CEO of Bull Outdoor Products and the bestselling author of *Pocket Mentor*

I have admired Jim's leadership style for a long time. He has the unique ability to be kind and tough at the same time, always keeping the vision in mind without losing touch with operational realities. When you read this book, you will understand that his success is not simply superior intuition and talent, but the result of a reflective and evidence-driven approach to leadership.

Soeren Mattke | Research Professor of Economics, University of Southern California

https://jimwetrich.com/stifled-checklist

ALSO BY JAMES G. WETRICH

Quitless: The Power of Persistence in Business and Life

STIFLED

Where Good Leaders Go Wrong

JAMES G. WETRICH

Leaders Press

Leaders Press

Published in the United States by Leaders Press.
www.leaderspress.com

ISBN 978-1-63735-045-4 (pbk)
ISBN 978-1-63735-038-6 (Amazon pbk)
ISBN 978-1-63735-044-7 (e-book)

Library of Congress Control Number: 2021901942

DEDICATION

To my family from whom there is endless support,
inspiration, and love

To those I have been so very fortunate to lead

To those leaders noted in the Appendix who nurtured me,
guided me, developed me, and most importantly, tolerated me

CONTENTS

FOREWORD

We had the pleasure of working with Jim Wetrich (aka Big Red) close to fifteen years ago while he was excelling as the president of the Americas for Mölnlycke Health Care (the highest performing division in this global, international corporation owned by Investor AB) and as a top tier executive MBA student at Goizueta Business School at Emory University in Atlanta. Graduating with top honors, Jim was a passionate student and practitioner of leadership and pursued every opportunity to develop and fine-tune his leadership skills and help others do the same. So, it was not a surprise when several years after his graduation from Goizueta when he was selected to be an Inaugural Fellow at Stanford's Distinguished Careers Institute in 2015. Jim further expanded and deepened his leadership experience by following his impressive corporate career in the health care and medical device industry by exercising his entrepreneurial skills and acquiring, building, and leading a consulting enterprise as well as a boutique health care outplacement, coaching, assessment, and search firm.

Jim's colleagues, peers, friends, and former faculty have encouraged him for many years to capture the lessons of his vast and varied leadership experience—an array of experiences that spans industries, geographic borders, hierarchical and functional roles. This book, *Stifled*, is the product of this exceptional leader who has demonstrated a capacity for what we would call "synthetic intelligence," a kind of wisdom that makes it possible to operate with a "both/and" mentality, balancing opposing possibilities and imperatives to achieve superior performance. Jim's leadership skills and big picture perspective have also made it possible for him to simultaneously balance the "polarities" of the business, i.e., dealing with both short-term *and* long-term trade-offs, maintaining a local focus *and* global perspective, and integrating strategic effectiveness with tactical efficiency. In its essence, *Stifled* is a collection of critical leadership lessons drawn from the breadth and depth of Wetrich's extensive experience.

In reading this book we are struck by Jim's leadership mindset—the faith and values he brings to the task of leading. Jim's underlying belief is that human beings and their organizations are driven by a fundamental desire to grow, learn, and achieve. As Erik Erikson, one of the founding fathers of developmental psychology, once wrote, "The plan for growth is all there if we will but let it live."

If we accept the basic premise of this book—that leaders are organizational servants whose primary task is to identify and liberate talent—a compelling logic emerges; namely, that the key leadership imperative is identifying and removing the barriers and impediments that block the full expression of human and organizational potential. *Stifled* provides the reader with an invaluable protocol that identifies seventeen critical impediments that derail leaders while also identifying the crucial opportunities that a leader must focus on to optimize organizational performance by building liberating day-to-day work environments and energizing positive cultures to promote human thriving.

Roderick Gilkey, Professor in the Practice of Organization & Management, Goizueta Business School, Emory University, Atlanta GA

Charles Goetz, Senior Lecturer Organization & Management, Goizueta Business School, Emory University, Atlanta, GA

INTRODUCTION

America's organizations are being stifled, and the cost is in the billions. But there is a lot we can do about the situation. We are on the heels of a global pandemic and in a prime position to make very effective changes. But rather than get back to "normal," we need to create a new normal where archaic mindsets and outdated practices no longer stifle us. We need to reexamine and overhaul virtually every aspect of our organizations.

I know this because I have over three decades of diverse experience in leadership positions at some of the world's largest and most successful companies. I've worked in the United States, Europe, and Latin America and successfully launched products on three continents. From my corporate and consulting work, I have firsthand experience with the practices of organizations of all sizes. I watched as people, profits, and innovation were stifled, often needlessly.

In this book, I will address the major issues organizations are now facing. The good news is that much of this can be relatively easy to implement, and we have the perfect opportunity to do so. With the outbreak of the pandemic, businesses and organizations worldwide have been forced to adapt or die. New tools and technology are being used that will allow or force many stiflers to be neutralized.

One critical issue I see facing the current crop of managers and leaders is that traditional management models don't work well with our newest generation of workers. Trying to enforce conventional models on these future leaders can be a disaster because they often know better. There's a lot to learn from them. But there is still much they need to learn from the old guard, so we should learn to communicate with them effectively.

As online technology and the recent pandemic have forced our hands, we are more global than ever. Old myopic leadership models no longer work, and many companies are failing because they cannot, or will not, adapt. They refuse to acknowledge the dramatic and rapid changes taking place. This negates their ability to pass on their knowledge and experience to younger generations—timeless knowledge only learned through experience that has been centuries in the making. Many young leaders are wasting valuable time and money reinventing the wheel. This book will examine the tried-and-true organizational management methods and suggest strategies for retaining the value while removing the stiflers.

In the present, and looking forward, the new workplace demands that people work independently and creatively. Remote work and video meetings are the norm. Teams span multiple countries and cultures. There's no more room for missteps and blunders in management. Layers of bureaucracy, micromanagers, and pointless meetings can no longer be tolerated if we want to keep our organizations competitive in the modern marketplace.

Let's tear apart the old ways and bring all that value to the table and merge it with the new. One thing I've discovered is that even with all these changes in the world, doing right and being ethical is still good business.

Considering and adopting new technologies and approaches to business is not knuckling under to cancel culture, social justice warriors, or the thought police; you are smartly incorporating the changing global workforce and adapting to the new workplace.

WHAT'S IN THE BOOK?

I BROKE THIS BOOK DOWN INTO every area that my experience, teaching, and research have shown me needs to be addressed. I came away with seventeen chapters.

Chapter One: Focus on Failure

Learning from our mistakes is age-old wisdom. Still, all too often, we see people trying to hide or pass off their mistakes. A good system that takes the good with the bad will teach us much. Learning from our failures is a critical skill in life and business. When you coach people to admit and learn from their mistakes rather than punishing them, they will learn to trust you and improve themselves and the organization they are part of.

Chapter Two: Clarity and Transparency

Clarity and transparency build trust and are critical elements to any thriving enterprise. Without these two elements, employees become disengaged to some degree. A disengaged employee is toxic to your organization. These employees are psychologically unattached to the company and contribute the minimum required of them; far worse, they spread their misery and dissatisfaction. Don't let these cancerous employees take hold of your organization. Instead, start with the root cause and foster an environment of clarity and transparency.

Chapter Three: Workplace Incivility and Bullying

Workplace incivility and bullying can take on many forms and can sometimes be unconscious. But, whether conscious or not, these behaviors can lead to some of the most significant organizational stiflers. Losing productivity can be the least of your worries as situations surrounding incivility and bullying can escalate into lawsuits and serious damage across an organization and the reputation of the company.

Chapter Four: Growth Mindset Versus Fixed Mindset

When you understand the growth mindset, you will see how things operate—how beliefs you might have assumed were carved in stone, when changed, can lead to an avalanche of new thoughts and actions that will change the trajectory of your life for the better.

Chapter Five: Self-Awareness

The importance of self-awareness in leadership and management cannot be overstated. Developing self-awareness is a large undertaking, but the rewards of being self-aware are worth the effort. Being aware of the perspective from which you operate, your worldview as formed based on your upbringing and experiences will make you a far better leader. You most likely won't view the world the same as the people you oversee, which can create issues that range from simple miscommunication to possibly offending someone.

Chapter Six: Hypocritical Leadership

Lead openly and honestly as the appearance of hypocrisy can be damaging. Management will do what they need to do for the business; they will make exceptions to the rules. What's important is that the reasons for these actions need to be made clear to everyone. An open and honest culture where we understand that exceptions will be made for the better of the business is acceptable; hypocritical leadership is not. Things are not always black and white, so let's not pretend they are.

Chapter Seven: Micromanagement and Design by Committee

Dealing with people is hard. Managing them is even harder. Dealing with them during the design process can be harder still.

You will have people with a lot to say and those that don't like to speak at all. But the volume of the words coming out of a person's mouth shouldn't be an indicator of the value of what they have to offer—effectively managing any process that can mutate into micromanaging or design by committee takes self-awareness, people skills, and excellent communication.

Chapter Eight: Management by Negativity

A negative manager focuses on problems and not solutions. They almost always offer the stick and not the carrot. As a result, the environment in the workplace becomes severely de-energized. A manager with a negative approach has great difficulty making improvements, and any improvement is likely the result of fear. Thus, fear-based management is ineffective long term.

Chapter Nine: Meetings

Meetings can be necessary, but they have become one of the most significant drains on businesses and organizations. Examine your approach to meetings, make changes, and remove one of the biggest stiflers that exist.

Chapter Ten: Bureaucracy

Large companies come with incredible resources and opportunities—and usually a bureaucracy. Bureaucracy has its uses, but it makes it very difficult to make progress and get work done when applied too heavily. Stifling bureaucracies are out-of-date, often unnecessary, and full of redundant policies that require mountains of paperwork. They spawn red tape and often operate on mindless rigid conformity. They can be breeding grounds for some of the worst problems an organization can face, yet they are essential to the functioning of an organization.

Chapter Eleven: Performance Reviews

We're in the midst of a revolution. The pace of the marketplace and the nature of the work demands that we develop people and give them feedback immediately. The old management paradigm of annual targets and performance reviews is obsolete. The need for ongoing coaching is now not only practical but vitally necessary. Younger generations want to grow, learn, and develop in their careers. They want to stay relevant, useful, and up to date on technology and trends. They will do this largely on their own and can be a great asset to whatever organization they belong to.

Chapter Twelve: The Servant Leader

Successfully implementing and practicing servant leadership can be a hard road to start down, but the benefits are immense and well worth the effort. Trusted employees, who've earned that trust, are inspired to be more trustworthy. As a result, the leader will give them more trust, and they will flourish. The leader that can do this will be the captain of a boat where all crew members are happily rowing in the same direction with all they've got.

As Stephen Covey says, "Trust is one of the means to achieve servant leadership, and it is also an end that is achieved by servant leadership."

Chapter Thirteen: Workplace Politics

Dealing with workplace politics can be nasty and problematic at all levels. Still, it must be done, or things will only get worse in your career or organization. Remember to be clear about the difference between advancement dependent on unethical or illegal criteria and simply dealing with office politics. Most important, you should never tolerate any demeaning, unethical, or illegal treatment.

Chapter Fourteen: Training

Poor or inadequate training can have myriad negative effects from unsafe working conditions, legal considerations, reduced productivity, increased turnover, to customer dissatisfaction—just to name a few. Training is critical. The price of not properly training people is far more significant than the cost of the training. Employees are an investment and not an expense.

Chapter Fifteen: Managing Leadership Transitions in the Workplace

Change or transition in the workplace makes people insecure, or at the least, they are left with many questions. They wonder if the change is for the better, what promises will be kept, and how the changes will affect them. It is critical that we know how to manage change now more than ever. Already there has been a massive amount of change thrust upon us in the last year. We are seeing a lot of people changing jobs, starting new positions, and even embarking on new careers.

Chapter Sixteen: Managing the Modern Workplace

Leading and managing in the coming years is going to be different. Things are already very different due to the pandemic, rapidly evolving technology, and the newer generation of millennials. There will be many challenges, and challenges always bring opportunities.

Chapter Seventeen: Management Postpandemic

There's no denying that the pandemic has had a dramatic impact on all of us and in so many ways. Virtually every person around the globe has been affected one way or the other. Whether it's changes in work environments, management, culture, society—our organizations will never be the same.

*

I hope you enjoy this book. If you have any questions or comments, please visit www.jimwetrich.com.

CHAPTER ONE

Focus On Failure

"The only real mistake is the one from which we learn nothing."

—Henry Ford

MUCH HAS BEEN WRITTEN ABOUT LEARNING from our mistakes. Unfortunately, many people still haven't gotten the point. Instead, they are actively engaged in trying to cover up their mistakes, or they're busy beating other people over the head with theirs. While people need to take responsibility for the consequences of their actions, I like to take a more holistic approach and take the good with the bad—we can learn from both. Sometimes a big mistake provides a priceless learning opportunity.

Most of us are reared in a school system where mistakes are recorded as part of our permanent record. They are labeled as failures, and we get this sense that our failures are stacking up in numbers far greater than our successes. As we move through the system, it can feel like a mountain made of failures is amassing behind us as we make yet more mistakes. As adults, we may feel that we have a history of many mistakes instead of a history of valuable lessons learned.

This process may be devastating; a child should never consider a bad grade on a test as a failure. It needs to be approached as an opportunity to learn. The only real failure is failing to learn from our experiences, successful or not. It is vital for school-aged children, especially, that they learn what caused the poor performance. Traditionally, it was assumed that the student simply didn't study enough. We are starting to understand there can be many reasons for low grades, from medical issues to social problems.

Because of this typical developmental process, many adults roll along in life feeling bad about themselves and repeating the same mistakes. Sometimes, we might get lucky and be diagnosed with an issue we can learn from or figure out a better way to study. But historically, students have been labeled as "not too bright" or "just not good with numbers." We become adults adverse to making a mistake—every choice, every decision must be the right one the first time or you get a big red X. But life doesn't work that way. Many successful people can tell you the inevitability of mistakes and failures and the value of the lessons learned from those so-called failures. I am still learning from the mistakes I make.

In the 1800s, Samuel Smiles, a Scottish author and government reformer, said, "We learn wisdom from failure much more than from success. We often discover what will do, by finding out what will not do; and probably he who never made a mistake never made a discovery." It has been altered and shortened over the years. Smiles believed that progress came from attitude and not law. Maybe it's time to change our commonly accepted paradigm that a mistake is a bad thing that people need to be punished for.

To not accept our mistakes and learn from them is the greatest mistake of all.

We can learn from an array of sources too. While this is a business-oriented book, we can learn and apply lessons from other people's failures, destructive behaviors, or terrible leadership across many disciplines. We talk about learning agility later in the book, and that is along those lines. Learning agility means you can digest large amounts of information and determine what is important. You can then utilize what you've learned in other unrelated areas.

The book *Accidents in North American Climbing 2020* by the American Alpine Club examines mountain climbing accidents in North America. You might think that the consequences of a poorly worded contract versus a poorly tied knot while mountain climbing would cause a vastly different approach to learning from our mistakes. You would think that climbers would take learning from their mistakes seriously. Let's take a look at this.

The first thing that jumped out at me is that some of these climbing accidents happen repeatedly. I am talking about life and death, fatal accidents. With the stakes being as high as they are in mountain climbing, you would think there would be a very serious attempt to learn from their mistakes. But learning from their mistakes is inadequately adopted by mountain climbers, even after decades of experience and hundreds of deaths. Despite the best efforts of the American Alpine Institute with the publication of *Accidents,* hoping they will save lives, people are still dying from fatal repeated mistakes.

Although the comparison of leadership and management to mountain climbing seems dramatic, the stakes are still high enough that the lessons learned from failed climbs can be easily applied to business. Studying what not to do must also be part of the conversation of what to do.

Another thing I noticed is that it is usually the smallest mistakes that have the most significant consequences. In climbing, it often comes down to one little knot. Dougald MacDonald, writer for the *Recreational Equipment Incorporated (REI) Blog* and the *American Alpine Institute Blog,* comments on the mistakes that cause climbing accidents year after year. He points out that trained climbers still fall. It is often failing to tie a simple stopper knot at the end of their rope—climbers are literally sliding off the end of their ropes and falling to their deaths. Inexperience causes some of these accidents, but there are still far too many people dying to excuse the failures.

This simple yet life-saving knot is a lesson that is translatable to management and leadership. It is often the smallest details, the most basic edicts of business, that trip us up. Things like don't sign anything until you read it, document everything, and so many other fundamentals that people still forget, overlook, or ignore.

There's also a problem with people grossly overestimating their ability. Two psychologists developed a hypothesis called The Dunning–Kruger effect that states that people with low abilities often overestimate those abilities. The concept of knowing what you don't know and accepting that you may not even know what you don't know is essential.

People get overconfident in mountain climbing and business. Fortunately, in business, it rarely leads to a fatality. But the consequences can be disastrous nonetheless.

Consequences of Poor Leadership

I'll call him Larry (not his real name).

I have to start by saying that I've been surrounded by and worked for outstanding managers and leaders since I began my career in 1981. I've worked for at least fifteen managers, every one of whom became an officer in a public or private company or a CEO. I've worked for some incredible people and learned much (see the appendix for a list).

And then there's Larry.

Larry was, without a doubt, the worse leader I've ever worked with. He had no idea the impact his decisions had on the business as a whole, and he didn't seem to care. He spouted slogans and buzzwords, but he was duplicitous and ingenuine. He lacked integrity.

He espoused the servant leadership model; he promoted trust, integrity, and honesty as the foundation of his "results pyramid." But he routinely lied, went back on his word, and was a terrible steward of the company's resources.

Larry did a much better job at managing up than down. He once sold a project to senior leadership, then failed to support the project within the company by not providing data, time, and resources. In several instances, Larry and his team didn't show up at important meetings that had been set up as a direct result of his efforts.

He never seemed to understand that how one division operates impacts all the other divisions, customers, and the company as a whole. Things that may irritate a customer may impact another division's ability to do its job. The customer doesn't see divisions; they see the company. A leader within a division of a company must understand that their actions have consequences beyond their sphere of influence and beyond their own division.

A Gallup poll of more than one million US workers concluded that the number one reason people quit their job is a bad boss or supervisor. There's also an interesting article in the October 2016 *Harvard Business Review,* "Why Leadership Training Fails—and What to Do About It."[1] Here's a quote from that article.

> "Overcoming Barriers to Change.
>
> In our work helping managers have honest conversations about the effectiveness of their organizations, we hear about six common barriers. Companies consistently struggle with
>
> (1) unclear direction on strategy and values, which often leads to conflicting priorities;
> (2) senior executives who don't work as a team and haven't committed to a new direction or acknowledged necessary changes in their own behavior;
> (3) a top-down or *laissez-faire* style by the leader, which prevents honest conversation about problems;
> (4) a lack of coordination across businesses, functions, or regions due to poor organizational design;

---

[1] Michael Beer, Magnus Finnström, and Derek Schrader, "Why Leadership Training Fails-and What to Do about It," *Harvard Business Review*, September 9, 2016, https://hbr.org/2016/10/why-leadership-training-fails-and-what-to-do-about-it.

(5) inadequate leadership time and attention given to talent issues; and
(6) employees fear telling the senior team about obstacles to the organization's effectiveness."

Those points support why people leave. When times are good, the impact that the direct supervising manager has is critical. In his book *Work Rules,* Laszlo Bock explains how Google has dealt with some of these situations. Google deliberately takes power and authority over employees away from managers. Here's an example of that in action.

Managers at Google cannot make unilateral decisions about hiring, firing, performance ratings, salaries, bonuses, internal awards and recognition, promotions, final product designs, and launch times. A group, a committee, or an independent team makes these decisions. Google is attempting to remove biases, favoritism, nepotism, and many things that often stifle an organization. Google, with its more team-based approach, has removed an incredible number of harmful practices that lead to people getting positions they shouldn't have.

Keep in mind that what works for Google may not be practical in other companies and organizations. There are certain situations where things have to be very prescriptive for health and safety reasons. In areas such as health care and hazardous materials, employees need to be told what to do. Obviously, there are many situations where extensive education and training is required.

Many professions require people to pass board exams, acquire certifications, and demonstrate high levels of competency to practice them. A CPA, for example, must pass a multipart assessment to put the initials CPA after their name. In addition, they must understand the nuances involved with tax reporting and accounting. But not managers.

The skills required to be a manager are complex and come from a mix of cognitive capabilities, learning, and emotional intelligence. Companies use various processes to measure these, but there's no specific proven assessment to predict which individuals will make a great manager or effective leader. Some companies have tried, but the complexity is daunting. Over time, neuroimaging and other technologies will help create predictive models that will aid us. Meanwhile, training and structural considerations have shown to be useful. Simulations, assessment centers, and the like are being adopted for medical education, which may also prove helpful for real-time challenges. Part of the challenge of training is simulating real stress. The military runs simulated combat drills. Part of SEAL training is all about functioning during stressful situations—they use live ammo in some exercises. It's hard to simulate those types of conditions safely and ethically. A manager may function fine until put into a stressful situation. People thrive in different environments, so that makes it complicated.

Determining the most important skills for any situation is another challenge. Again, different companies will have different needs and environments. Larger firms often use scale to track this over time; smaller firms don't have the infrastructure necessary to do this.

Managerial Expectations

It is important to understand the managerial processes within an organization. These roles will vary widely among corporations and are not always effectively organized. A manager's responsibilities are often ambiguous, and that ambiguity is fertile ground for stifling behaviors, be it conscious or unconscious. Transparency can help with this issue.

Judy Faulkner, founder and CEO of Epic, one of the largest electronic health record technology providers in the United States, if not the world, claims they have the most comprehensive employee screening and testing of any company. Moreover, the results of those assessments are available to everyone in the organization. She believes this transparency is essential and highly beneficial to the employees and the company.

This approach allows for the effective use of all the skills and talents within the organization. Epic has built an incredibly successful multibillion-dollar business, so this seems to work for them.

Again, what may work for one company may not work for others.

Most companies perform what they call a postmortem, which is aptly named because a postmortem is the examination of a dead body. Sometimes we hear this process called an After-Action Review (ARR), but that's actually incorrect. There's a critical difference between the two.

The military pioneered the ARR, a review that takes place after each step of a battle. It is a continuous, almost instantaneous process that happens skirmish after skirmish. It is feedback and improvement on the fly. Just like mountain climbing, the stakes in battle are life and death. There's no waiting around for a dead body to examine because the corpse might end up being yours. You can see how each approach would yield different results. In business, like in battle, you can't afford to wait around until the end to assess and make adjustments.

When your life is on the line, it is easier to speak your mind. However, it's challenging to get useful information in business because people are often afraid to speak up, especially in groups. This is directly related to the environment created by management. If people are asking questions like this, you have stifled employees: "Can I really trust my manager?" "Will so-and-so take this as a personal attack and try to get back at me?" If they are concerned with petty politics and egos at the table and fear drives their behavior, you have a problem.

I've worked internationally, spending over a quarter of my career at Scandinavian firms. One of the most significant faults I've seen in US companies is that people tend to personalize things much more than they do in other countries, particularly European countries.

Americans take feedback as a personal criticism. This goes back to that mindset that you are a failure if you don't get it right the first time. Feedback regarding how you can make something better (because it's not already perfect) is perceived by some as a red X on their work. An American may perceive that the person who gives them feedback must not like them. This causes a schism, and suddenly everything is seen as black or white, right or wrong, good or bad. This destroys the opportunity for open and honest debate. I've seen the feedback process at non-US-based companies where it's considered vital to have your feelings known.

Safe and honest feedback and debates where all opinions are heard and considered only exist in a healthy work environment. It needs to be taught and fostered in American businesses.

I came across a review written in 2016 called *Assessment and Development of Global Leadership Competencies in the Workplace, a Review of Literature.*[2] The authors listed seventeen personality characteristics consistently linked to effective global leadership.

1. Adaptability; flexibility
2. Agreeableness
3. Conscientiousness
4. Cultural sensitivity
5. Emotional intelligence (EQ)
6. Extraversion; sociability
7. Inquisitiveness; curiosity
8. Open-mindedness
9. Openness to experience
10. Optimism
11. Resilience
12. Self-awareness; self-confidence
13. Self-efficacy
14. Stability; stress tolerance; low neuroticism
15. Tolerance for ambiguity
16. Tenacity
17. Values; integrity; character

[2] Denise Cumberland, Ann Herd, Meera Alagaraja, and Sharon Kerrick, "Assessment and Development of Global Leadership Competencies in the Workplace: A Review of Literature," *Advances in Developing Human Resources* (May 2016).

If you asked a prospective employee to take seventeen assessments to test those characteristics, they'd probably tell you they were busy. These seventeen characteristics are just a few aspects of what makes a good manager. There's knowledge, technical skills, and other competencies. It's daunting. There are numerous assessments available on the market, but there's no comprehensive, organized tool for this. There are so many elements to being an effective manager that it's almost impossible to assess. It's what makes being a good manager so challenging.

Behavioral Interviewing

Many companies have moved to behavioral interviewing. I like this approach. They typically present many scenarios and ask how you would handle each situation. It's the closest thing to SEAL training we have.

Another helpful tool is getting a wide variety of opinions from other employees at the company. So much of what makes someone successful is how well they fit into a company's culture.

It can be challenging to bring skills from one company into another that operates entirely differently. For example, a person may perform well in a command-and-control organization, but they may fail in a team-based environment like Google.

*

> Learning from our mistakes is age-old wisdom. Still, we all too often see people trying to hide or pass off their mistakes. A system that takes the good with the bad will teach us much. Learning from our failures is a critical skill in life and business. When you coach people to admit and learn from their mistakes rather than punish them, they will learn to trust you, and they will improve themselves and the organization of which they are a part.

CHAPTER TWO

Clarity And Transparency

> "The single most important ingredient in the recipe for success is transparency because transparency builds trust."
>
> —Denise Morrison

A GREAT STIFLER OF PRODUCTIVITY IN an organization is a lack of clarity and transparency from upper management. Although these are two different issues, they overlap, so I'd like to look at them together.

Given the recent events in the world, the pandemic being the biggest disruptor, the business landscape for managers and leaders has become very unclear. As people have been forced online en masse, they have become more aware, more knowledgeable, and as a result, some have become more skeptical. They are far more demanding and want to know more about the companies they work for and do business with. Customers and vendors want to know where and how their products are made. People around the world are interested in the ethical and environmental impacts their support and purchases have on our world.

Employees are no exception as they want a greater level of transparency in the business they work for. A paycheck is no longer the motivator it once was—people want to know what the mission and goals of a company are. They want to know how the organization views issues and what they are doing about those issues. And now, the actual work environment—work from home, in the office, or a hybrid—is of key concern and consideration.

Business transparency is crucial to building trust among your customers, employees, vendors, and all the individuals that fuel your business. I will say it many times throughout this book—trust is critical. Trust is the foundation of a successful business of any size, and that trust is hard to build and easy to lose today.

Harvard Business Review Analytic Services (HBRAS) surveyed nearly 800 executives worldwide, and they cited three crucial barriers to achieving greater transparency in organizations: technical transparency, organizational transparency, and cultural transparency.

Cultural transparency is when employees feel heard. Employees also like to be aware of what the leaders of the organization are like. They want to be led by example.

Technical transparency is making sure that everyone in your organization has the tools and the training to access information about the organization and the ability to communicate with others in the organization.

Organizational transparency is making sure that people know things like who owns the company, where and how the products are made, how certain issues are viewed and handled, and a lot more. People want to know what they are supporting.

There are a few highlights from the HBRAS study, such as 90 percent of executives say increased business transparency leads to better-informed decision-making across the entire organization, 55 percent say that ethical and commercial considerations are equally important when evaluating suppliers, and 26 percent say transparent finance and procurement processes would lead to cost reductions from 11 to 20 percent. [3]

Transparency is about being honest and straightforward. Transparent management is about sharing information and encouraging questions to clarify and understand what is presented. When a mistake is made, it is examined openly and honestly. While consequences may befall some people, the goal isn't to punish. When management operates transparently, employees feel trusted and invested, a solid reputation is built, and most important, you reduce employee turnover and increase productivity. Transparency builds trust, and that is of utmost import.

In our technological age, it's almost impossible to get ahead of a story to do damage control. It's better not to lie or bend the truth—word will spread globally almost instantly if you are caught. Customers today are tuned in to many sources of information pertaining to their needs and interests. A bum product that gets shipped once may well end up on a video that goes viral with the truth about the product within hours of its release. The same goes for employees and past employees. There are sites where employees can evaluate their past jobs and the bosses at those companies. High turnover due to poor management or other practices cannot be hidden and will greatly reduce the quantity and the quality of your potential talent pool.

You don't want to be foolish and release the organization's most sensitive and valuable information for the public to see. More transparency also means more caution. You will want to make sure you are protecting whatever you are sharing, which leads us to clarity. You also want to be very clear on the who, what, when, where, and why of the information you are sharing.

A lack of organizational clarity is a recipe for disaster. We need to be very clear in all of our communications, whether it's a simple

---

[3] Basware, "Using Transparency to Enhance Reputation and Manage Business Risk," https://www.basware.com/en-en/resources/harvard-business-review-analytic-services-using-tr."

office memo or a marketing campaign. With employees, we need to be very clear about the goals and mission of the company.

Everything should be clearly stated and reviewed by multiple sources to ensure clarity. This is particularly challenging in global companies where words don't have a direct translation and may be nuanced. In addition, a nomenclature or vocabulary should be adopted and used consistently to ensure clarity. There are so many acronyms these days that it is easy to get confused. For example, AP can mean access point, Asia-Pacific, Atlantic Pacific, accounts payable, or advanced placement, depending on the context.

This is particularly true when senior executives address the company. They often use internal terms that have little or no understanding to the broad audience. Your "August Update" (part of the company's annual financial planning system) may have no relevance to entry-level employees below senior management.

Having managers and leaders live by what they espouse is another way to ensure clarity. For example, no profanity might be a written rule, but if the manager swears like a sailor, it can lead to confusion. The assumption will be that the rule doesn't really matter. And if that rule can be broken without penalty, what other rules can we break?

Clarity means simplicity and consistency. When simplicity isn't an option for a complex contract, massive amounts of documentation, or other such communication, steps must be taken to ensure an understanding by all. Well-written summations and presentations are recommended in these situations.

A recent Gallup poll concluded that 14 percent of employees are "actively disengaged," and as high as 54 percent are "not engaged."[4] It's essential to understand the difference between the two. An "engaged employee" is highly involved in, enthusiastic about, and committed to their work and the workplace. An

[4] Jim Hartner, "Historic Drop in Employee Engagement Follows Record Rise," Gallup, July 2, 2020, https://www.gallup.com/workplace/313313/historic-drop-employee-engagement-follows-record-rise.aspx.

"actively disengaged" worker is miserable and actively spreads their misery around the workplace. They are corporate cancer.

So, we have more than half of workers not engaged—as high as 54 percent. These people are psychologically unattached to their work and company, meaning they put in the time, but they don't do it with energy or passion. They typically contribute the minimum effort required and are usually on the lookout for a better job. They will quickly take any job that comes along that is slightly better. They are also an easy target for the actively disengaged who are looking for company. Misery loves company.

This means that our workplaces are filled with primarily dissatisfied and disengaged people, even people who actively spread their dissatisfaction and do further damage. These employees mostly don't trust their leaders. The root cause is primarily due to a lack of clarity and transparency.

Employee Engagement

I have been fortunate that I haven't had to endure situations like this in the places I've worked, but I know it's a real problem. We didn't measure employee engagement until later in my career, and I know how critical it can be. It's common sense to me.

Employee engagement by itself is not an end-all. Still, this data can be used in conjunction with other assessments to develop an overall evaluation of the work environment and the extent to which employees are satisfied. A satisfied and engaged employee can empower and inspire those around them. Having an actively disengaged employee in your midst is self-sabotage. Unlike other stifling behaviors, this one is easy to fix.

Employee satisfaction and engagement are critical to the positive performance of a business. My professor at Emory University, Rick Gilkey, who became a mentor and a friend, came up with an excellent analogy for this situation. I embellished it a little for clarity.

Imagine a rowing crew where only half of the rowers work as hard as possible and are engaged and cooperative. They understand and support the mission, trust the captain, and care about the team. But the other half rows halfheartedly, and there's even a person in the back letting their oar drag in the water! They're talking loudly, complaining, and questioning everything the captain does. They wonder out loud why the race is important; as a result, they sow doubt into a few of the team members. A couple on their side of the boat is distracted, and their rowing slacks off even more. This is what an actively disengaged team member can do. Not only would this boat lose a race, but it would go in circles. This situation is a result of poor leadership and a lack of clarity. It would have been better if half the team had not even boarded the boat. With the reduced team size, they might have gone in the right direction, but they would still not have had the power to win a race. OK, enough embellishment.

Mission Reexamined

Another big stifler in a company happens when employees don't understand its vision or mission and their role in achieving that goal. What is it about the work I am doing as an individual that is important? Many employees cannot provide the simple context of their work. It's often not well communicated from the beginning. Currently, there's a significant shift going on, and American companies are reexamining their mission.

In the past, the mission of a company was simple: to maximize profits for the stakeholders. Recently, the Business Roundtable was formed. The Business Roundtable is an association of CEOs from America's most successful companies promoting a thriving US economy while expanding opportunity for all Americans through sound public policy. A number of CEOs have already signed on to this. They recognize that the mission of a business cannot be only about profits anymore. Other issues are important to the organization, and we see a shift away from the pure profit model.

What's most important is that the employees understand the mission, goals, and organization values. Most companies are not just about capitalism anymore, and a meaningful mission can't be summed up in a pithy mission statement. This makes it critical that managers and leaders can explain to their people why they are rowing the boat. Why should they be invested and give their all to win the race? Many employees don't even know why they are there other than a paycheck. It's very disengaging when people don't understand why they're doing what they are doing, even if they are getting paid to do it.

Communicating Mission

It starts at the very beginning, even before people are hired to work for an organization. Everyone needs to understand exactly what the organization is trying to achieve. They also need to clearly understand all that will be expected of them. Work hours, flexibility, and environment all need to be transparent and communicated upfront.

An acquaintance who works for a European firm has a team conference call every Thursday. The fact that Thanksgiving in America falls on a Thursday every year means nothing to the European firm. Scheduling a significant event like a company conference call on Thanksgiving is as disengaging and demotivating as it gets. It's one of the most important holidays in the United States. I have also seen European-based companies have global meetings on July 4, insisting on participation from US colleagues.

The American-based companies I worked for never insisted on representation from any person outside of the US when it conflicted with a major national holiday in their country. So, it was stifling regardless of whether it was a decision made of ignorance or a disregard of the importance of the holiday. It's disrespectful. It's demotivating. It's disengaging.

This rigid requirement also put my acquaintance in a problematic situation. He decided that he would not participate in the call but think of the pressure that put him under. Having to make that decision at all is detrimental to him in a number of ways—professionally, emotionally, etc. There should never be that kind of pressure in an organization, but these kinds of things happen all the time. If this practice were known upfront, it could have been handled, avoided, or otherwise dealt with. The manager responsible for the meeting could have simply moved it one day forward.

The point is my friend wasn't given a choice or the opportunity to avoid this difficult situation. Things like this are why people are stifled and why engagement scores are so abysmal. As my now-deceased friend Bob Parkinson, retired Chairman and CEO of Baxter International, used to say, "It's the simple stuff that is the hard stuff."

But employee engagement continues to be overlooked and even dismissed outright. Managers' salaries, or lack thereof, usually have nothing to do with employee engagement scores. They're paid to hit numbers, so by gosh, they're going to hit their numbers. And many managers don't even believe in the concept. The value of employee engagement is a ridiculous notion to them. They haven't embraced it because they don't understand it and don't care to try. Maybe it's time they do. If they could see the data on how employee engagement affects a company, I think they would jump on board. It's just good business.

Being a leader today is more complicated than ever. We've moved from an environment where command and control used to be the way things were done. Generally, standardized processes and procedures surrounded leaders. Things were cut and dried. But now, we find ourselves in environments where much of the work is knowledge work, and creativity has become crucial.

Twenty or thirty years ago, employees were told what to do, when to do it, and how to do it. Now companies are engaged in work where that is no longer the right way to lead. People need to be more independent, creative, and invested in getting the job done. In addition, there needs to be a much higher degree of transparency simply for the sake of speed and expediency. Companies can no longer afford to work at a snail's pace or wait for troubled employees to self-correct or be gone. This is essential.

In the past, creativity was stifled, and that practice is still largely in effect, but today the work is complex and creativity critical. It's a huge shift. Unfortunately, most leaders are not prepared to lead in such an environment. For many old-school managers, things like transparency make them seem vulnerable and disempowered.

The Gallup survey says that improving employee engagement starts with clarity among leaders and managers. And it's what we've been talking about, this notion of clarity.

Embrace Millennials

When my younger son was in his late twenties, he worked at an investment banking firm. My son is highly quantitatively oriented and very bright. He would go into his boss's office (a forty-something-year-old) to share his ideas and suggestions. One day the boss yelled at him, "Matt! Stop trying to innovate. Go back to your office and do the work we're asking you to do."

This is the kind of mishandled situation that is stifling organizations. Most older people don't know how to handle millennials. Their inclination is to rein them in and bend them to their will. When a millennial offers ideas, creativity, and new ways of looking at things in a traditional business environment, they usually get shut down. I tell my clients we need to water these young people and watch them grow. We can learn from them. We need to get the hell out of their way and stop trying to force them into an old mold.

Incidentally, my son left that firm and started his own company.

Transparency

Seventy-three percent of companies have decided that lying to employees about their potential to advance is the right choice. In a study referenced in *Leadership BS: Fixing Workplaces and Careers One Truth at a Time* by Jeffrey Pfeffer of Stanford, companies have apparently decided that telling people the truth about their actual promotion prospects will demotivate them, and turnover might increase. I happen to believe that transparency is the right thing for employees and employers.[5] Transparency was one thing I admired in Tim Ring. Tim worked briefly in human resources at Abbott Laboratories before his meteoric rise to Chairman and CEO of the medical device company C. R. Bard, Inc. Under his leadership, Bard thrived.

Tim believed that if there is information about you on file somewhere (feedback, comments, reviews, etc.), you should know about it and have access to that information. Once, when I was in his office in human resources at Abbott, he pulled a notebook off the shelf from the internal succession planning process. He opened it and said, "This is where people think you'll be in three to five years and the roles they see you in." Why shouldn't there be that transparency in every company?

I thought the feedback that pertained to me was quite reasonable. Knowing that feedback allowed me to make changes. I don't believe that information predicted my future, or it did less so after knowing what it said. I ended up leaving the division. I took a different turn than was predicted for me, but that feedback certainly helped open up opportunities.

What was most important was that I got to see where there might be gaps in my competencies and made changes. Closing those gaps was very beneficial to me. I got a lot out of that small, simple but extraordinary example of transparency.

*

Clarity and transparency build trust and are critical elements to any thriving enterprise. Without these two elements, employees become disengaged to a wide variety of degrees. A disengaged employee is toxic in your organization. These employees are psychologically unattached to the company and contribute the minimum required of them, and far

[5] Jeffrey Pfeffer, *Leadership BS: Fixing Workplaces and Careers One Truth at a Time*, (New York: Harper Business, 2015).

worse, they spread their misery and dissatisfaction. Don't let these cancerous employees take hold of your organization. Instead, start with the root cause and foster an environment of clarity and transparency.

CHAPTER THREE

Workplace Incivility And Bullying

"A person who is nice to you but rude to the waiter is not a nice person."

—Dave Barry

"May I stress the need for courageous, intelligent, and dedicated leadership. . .leaders of sound integrity. Leaders not in love with publicity but in love with justice. Leaders not in love with money but in love with humanity. Leaders who can subject their particular egos to the greatness of the cause."

—Martin Luther King, Jr.

Bullying and even simple incivility in the workplace can be a minefield of potentially serious problems. It must be dealt with, and it must be dealt with carefully. It is a very serious issue with serious ramifications. There is a guide at the end of this chapter to help you deal with bullying no matter how you may be experiencing it. It is also helpful to review to make sure that you are not inadvertently being a bully, supporting a bully, or overlooking one.

Workplace incivility and bullying can take on many forms. The person creating the situation may not even be aware of the effect their actions are having. Whether it's conscious or unconscious, these behaviors can lead to some of the most significant organizational stiflers and need to be dealt with.

It's especially important that we examine this topic because the loss of productivity can be the least of your worries as these situations can escalate into lawsuits and cause serious damage across an organization and even to the reputation of the company.

Let's start with incivility. Incivility is generally defined as rude or unsociable speech or behavior, being impolite. Organizations are people, and people can quickly get too comfortable; that's when they may use inappropriate and offensive language. Rarely does a day go by in a company that there isn't some incivility. It can be a bad habit of using colorful language, an attempt at humor, or an unchecked mood. It's most often not intentional. And as our workplaces get more diverse and global, we need to be extra careful about what we say and how we handle different situations. The results of any form of incivility can damage relationships.

In my observation, there's an assumption that people's skins are thicker than they really are. If the CEO uses the "F" bomb, people will assume it's OK for them to use it; they may even feel obligated to use it.

Today, we simply have to be much more sensitive to and cognizant of the fact that certain behaviors are more offensive to other countries and cultures. It makes sense that one group or culture is most likely unaware of what's offensive to a different group or culture, so we have to take extra effort and be more aware as we prepare ourselves and our organizations.

I don't think many managers' first concern is being well-mannered; there are many pressures and priorities on their plates. I'm not excusing ill-mannered behavior; I'm just pointing out why it might be overlooked, even scoffed at, by a busy manager in an organization. And that's my point. That's why I'm discussing it. When the real effects of incivility and bullying behavior are presented to a manager, I expect that they will embrace the need for change.

*

Bullying is generally targeted; it's when somebody goes after somebody else. It is generally considered to be much worse than incivility. This is largely due to the common perception of a bully who is a loud and threatening public aggressor. This perception leads many to think that bullying might be easy to identify, but this isn't always true. In fact, a person can be a bully in ways that are subtle and unseen.

According to HR.com, almost half of human resource professionals agree that their organization is positive and nontoxic, whereas a little more than half agree that negative stress is prevalent in the workplace.[6] This statistic stems from many things. Bullying can be physical, emotional, and psychological. I have been fortunate as I haven't seen many circumstances of bullying in the places I've worked. But one thing I have noticed that qualifies as bullying, and it's quite common, is where a manager or organization wants an employee gone, and they have no grounds for termination. Suddenly, the manager establishes unreasonable goals and objectives for that employee, knowing that they will fail. The employee was set up for failure, and the result was their

6 HR.com Limited, "Press Release: Hr Research Institute," Everfi and HR Research Institute HR Research Study," HR.com, November 26, 2019, https://www.hr.com/en/about_us/hr_com_press_releases/everfi-and-hr-research-institute-hr-research-study_k3g053zv.html?s=YRkzbPkik32TUzFdbP.

termination. This is a cowardly way to handle the situation and a horrible thing to do to a person.

Taking the easy way out often leads to a situation where someone is bullied. The hallmark of a good leader is to take decisive action, but increasing concerns over diversity and other sensitivities have created a lot of self-doubt in leaders and managers. They are almost bullied by the situation, especially if they are in any way different from the people they are managing. Avoiding confrontation because of the fear of being viewed as somehow intolerant or the fear of legal action is a surefire way to fail.

This discomfort and avoidance can lead to a very stifling backlash that creates the opposite effect of what was intended, where diversity is secretly frowned upon and actively avoided. Sometimes bullying can arise from the discomfort surrounding diversity. Let's touch on what diversity is and how to deal with it.

Understanding Diversity

Diversity in the US and many other countries has deep and very broad implications. There's gender identity, sexual orientation, religious affiliation (or lack of), race, and more. Some managers aren't comfortable discussing or dealing with diversity, but it needs to be dealt with effectively. I intend to explore the term in more detail to help managers with many backgrounds get a grip on what diversity means so they can effectively manage these situations. Here's just one example of why we need to explore and examine diversity—some still don't know what it means.

Once, when I was a senior leader at a company, a female employee asked the senior head of HR (also a woman) during a global conference of the company managers how our global company promoted diversity. Her answer illustrates the lack of awareness many managers have of the broad global implications of diversity. She said, "We're very diverse. We've got one executive from France, one from Austria, Sweden, the UK, America. . ." She thought diversity meant what countries people came from. This is definitely not the definition of diversity we have in the US.

Many female executives, and particularly those from the US, were displeased by her answer. Fast forward ten years now. The new CEO of that company boasted about the fact that the company now has as many women as men on the executive team (Bravo!). Alas, the photo on the LinkedIn post showed that they were all Caucasian (nice try, but not even close, once again).

People still fear diversity in the workplace. There can be many reasons for this but approaching it from a purely bottom-line perspective might be the best tactic. Diversity opens up your talent pool and your market. Diversity in your organization will help you navigate a world that increasingly demands it. Research by firms such as McKinsey & Company shows that diverse companies are more effective and profitable.

Admittedly, achieving diversity can be hard. While some managers are resistant, many are simply scared to death and have no idea what to say or do.

Bullying by Proxy

There is another horrible behavior I've seen. Sometimes, when an employee is about to get a large payout on their stock options and about to vest, they are terminated. The company doesn't want to have to make good on those options. I've also seen situations where managers are asked to reduce head count in the worst possible way. In one particular situation, a company leader asked a manager to reduce his organization by two hundred people.

The manager responded, "It's almost Thanksgiving. I'll work on a plan and get back to you in January."

The leader said, "No, I want this done now."

The manager replied, "But Christmas is in a couple of weeks. . ."

"If you can't get this done before Christmas, I'll find somebody who can," the leader replied as he abruptly hung up the phone.

The manager was bullied into doing an awful thing because his boss wanted the head count off the books by the end of the year.

If you have even a bit of a conscience, it's very difficult to lay people off. I've had to do it, and it was the worst experience in my entire life. It's absolutely gut-wrenching, and it's even worse if you are forced to do it during a challenging time. Getting laid off is never good, but getting laid off right before a holiday is even more difficult.

Unfortunately, most companies are still run on the premise that an employee has two choices: suck it up or leave.

Failure by management can lead to bullying

The Center for Creative Leadership concluded in one study that 50 percent of leaders were failures.[7] By failure, they meant that one of every two managers and leaders is estimated to be ineffective, which is defined by disappointment, incompetence, a misfire, or a complete failure in their current role.

In my opinion, this unacceptably high failure rate is due in large part to the fact that most managers and leaders are not well-trained or their training is generally short in duration. Usually, managers are left up to their own devices. They're thrown in the deep end and expected to swim. If we make our numbers, we're gold, which is a very shortsighted view. Managers are not coached, mentored, and supervised for as long and as closely as they should be. If they were, we could identify problems early on. We could modify the manager's behaviors and take a big step toward preventing trouble in the future. Ultimately, we would save a lot of money. *Preventing* employee disengagement, turnover, and lawsuits is far cheaper than having to deal with them.

Unless the workplace protects employees and allows them to provide feedback safely, they usually won't. They might even quit. Employee feedback is essential to heading off problems. If a safe

---

[7] William A. Gentry, Paige Logan, and Scott Tonidandel, "Understanding the Leadership Challenges of First-Time Managers," Transitioning Into Leadership Series, accessed September 16, 2021, https://cclinnovation.org/wp-content/uploads/2020/03/understandingleadershipchallenges.pdf

path for feedback is created for employees to point out such things as abusive behavior, companies could handle things earlier rather than later when the issues are still relatively minor.

People will gladly expose problems in an organization if they are safe when doing so. But if the organization's culture suppresses feedback or uses it against the employees, subordinates will fear retribution. It's like the captain of a ship punishing the sailor for pointing out an iceberg on the horizon. A slight adjustment sooner than later can have hugely beneficial effects and be so much less expensive.

Know thyself

Part of preventing yourself and others from creating a hostile workplace is being self-aware. Just because a company made you a manager doesn't mean you are necessarily going to be an effective manager. If you are rising up in an organization, that means you are good at something. You most likely have the knowledge, experience, and self-assurance to make decisions. But are you self-aware? The very confidence that propels us forward can sometimes lead to a blindness that holds us back.

It is easy to be blind to our faults and weaknesses or believe we need to hide them to survive the corporate world. It can be tough to expose yourself to honest examination, even private self-examination, but learning your blind spots and weaknesses is empowering.

So, you got the management job. You sense the pressure to live up to the expectations of the company. If things are not well-defined for you, you need to take time and sort things out about yourself, your team, and the organization.

Self-awareness is so critical that there is an entire chapter on it in this book. But let's look at it now briefly because being self-aware is an essential step in becoming a successful manager and leader. So, how do you become more self-aware? You can do many things to achieve this. Here's a shortlist to get you started.

- Practice mindfulness with activities such as meditation.

- Attempt to see yourself honestly and objectively.
- Journal: take notes about things that stand out to you.
- Ask for feedback from friends and colleges.
- Write down your dreams, goals, and plans.

This is a short list, but the one thing I've found that really helps me is to journal and take notes. I'm old-fashioned in many ways, although current in my skills. I still like pen and paper and use a notebook, called a black and red notebook. I write most my notes in that notebook. I've never made the transition to a completely digital world.

I try to capture things that are good and bad. I notate all kinds of things, both in a written journal and on my iPhone. I also keep a little black book where I take notes on things that are really important to me, things that have impacted me. For example, when I saw Margaret Thatcher give a speech in 2000, I kept the notes from that speech in my little black book, and occasionally I still read over them.

The act of writing can be pure catharsis. It's been helpful for me to capture both good and bad behaviors I've observed in myself and others. I like to take notes when I'm in a learning moment from a person or situation.

Over time, recollections fade. Our memories of a situation that may have been really important to us at the time can change. Sometimes it turns out that the thing I took note of wasn't really that important after all. But there's still value to have the notes to look back on and reflect. It's like rereading an old book and getting something new out of it each time. I've reread the first leadership book I've ever purchased many times. I bought *On Becoming a Leader* by Warren Bennis when it first came out in 1989, and every time I read it, I get something new out of it. I've changed, I've grown, I've matured, and his words impact me differently today than they did thirty years ago.

You can have that same impact on yourself by taking notes and looking back over them occasionally. This leads me to the reason for being self-aware—being true to yourself.

Be true to thyself

The most important thing in management and leadership, above everything else, is knowing who you are and what you believe. You must know what's important to you and what you stand for so you can make the many tough decisions that will be put before you.

I heard a story about Jim Lentz, president and CEO of Toyota of North America. I don't know Jim well; I've met him on a few occasions. Jim is a marvelous executive and leader. He worked for Toyota for a long time. He's a family-oriented individual, humble, and worked for one of the top ten largest companies in the world (Jim has recently retired). He's extremely grounded and down to earth. He's generous. I think you get the picture—Jim's a really great guy. This is pretty amazing for an executive at his level.

When Jim was a district manager in 1983, he faced a major decision. His manager called a team meeting to discuss the monthly sales results. As Jim reflects, "My manager pulled me aside and said I was too soft on people. He wanted me to change my style and motivate people with an iron fist. I told him that I had to be who I was, and I couldn't change that, nor could I commit to his demands. And he gave me two weeks to find another job."

This is the kind of pressure used to bully people that I was talking about earlier. Jim handled it by finding a new job at corporate headquarters in Southern California. He took a demotion and a pay cut, but he was true to himself. He made the right choice. He had the foresight to take the demotion and look at the long view, and he ended up running the North American operations. Many people confronted with a similar situation would have quit and left Toyota behind. Honestly, I probably would have.

There's no guarantee that being true to yourself will lead to you running Toyota of North America, but I've seen people in situations similar to Jim's that didn't walk away. Ultimately, they ended up in a worse situation than had they walked away. In some cases, staying and fighting led to the company going after them with retribution.

You have to know going in what's really important to you. You can't always bend to the rules of the organization. This is where many people get into trouble; they're asked to do things they know they shouldn't, but they do them because there's this unbelievable pressure from the people above them.

I check in with myself all the time. It is really important to set time aside for self-reflection. I've got my credo on my wall, right in front of my face. I read it every day.

Big Red's Personal Credo

Whomever you serve, serve them with caring and respect.

Whatever you do, do it with passion and integrity.

Whenever you reach, reach beyond your grasp.

Wherever you go, go as a leader.

Above all, have fun.

Steve Jobs used to go on long walks and think, but I'm sure he did some self-reflection and reflecting on those walks as well. It's also important to have good people around you, whether they're coaches, mentors, partners, or family members.

*

Workplace incivility and bullying can take on many forms and can sometimes be unconscious. But, whether conscious or not, these behaviors can lead to some of the most significant organizational stiflers. The loss of productivity can be the least of your worries as situations surrounding incivility and bullying can escalate into lawsuits and serious damage across an organization and the reputation of the company.

Bullying in the workplace, a guide for employees and managers

As defined earlier in this chapter, workplace bullying is usually verbal instead of the traditional image of a schoolyard bully that picks on the smaller kids. Although bullying can sometimes be a hostile physical act, it usually is more subtle and involves numerous smaller incidents. It's most often a pattern of intimidation that is usually conscious but can be unconscious as well. When a person is offended, degraded, or humiliated, they are being bullied, whether they appear to be or not. This is where it gets tricky for managers. How do you stop bullying that you aren't even aware is happening?

Any comments of conduct directed at an individual and based on a personal characteristic such as, but not limited to, race, creed, religion, color, sex, sexual orientation, marital status, family status, disability, physical size or weight, age, nationality, ancestry or place of origin, gender identity, or pregnancy can be considered bullying. Anything that should reasonably be known as unwelcome, such as sexual advances, sexually suggestive comments, jokes, gestures, inappropriate images, or any unwanted contact can be considered harassment.

In the workplace, simple comments can psychologically hurt a person. When this happens, they can feel isolated. The situation can deteriorate rapidly, often with no one being any the wiser, until a significant problem erupts, sometimes a lawsuit or even a news story.

Effectively dealing with bullying is in step with the latest trends in occupational health and safety laws. Employees are now often expected to anticipate and prevent bullying in their workplaces. It seems common sense to most managers that no one should work in an environment where they don't feel safe and comfortable, but that's not the issue. What's essential is covered in these guidelines, and that's the ability to identify and deal with bullying.

Bullying can be both obvious and subtle, but it is always an aggressive act. What might seem like harmless play to one person can be considered an aggressive act by another. Managing bullying requires that you do not judge the seriousness of a complaint, only that you deal with it properly.

The following isn't a comprehensive checklist; instead, it is the start of one. There is no way to list every incident that can be considered bullying, especially since bullying is very case-by-case in nature. Remember that bullying is usually a pattern of behavior, so you will need to watch and document any incidents that might occur.

Bullying can include:

- Overloading someone with work to cause an outcome
- Demeaning a person when they offer an opinion
- Preventing training that might lead to a promotion
- Denying leave without cause
- Changing guidelines to confuse or trip up
- Constant criticism; a no-win situation
- Making deadlines that are impossible; setting up a person to fail
- Excluding or isolating individuals, even socially.
- Any act of intimidation
- Being intrusive; harassing, snooping, or stalking
- Joking in a manner that is offensive by word or email
- Physical abuse of any kind
- Spreading rumors, gossiping, or making innuendo, even if not malicious
- Tampering with personal belongings
- Deliberately undermining a person
- Causing a person to feel useless in some fashion
- Undeserved or extreme punishment
- Giving false information, or withholding information, required for work
- Using profanity
- Yelling, screaming, and otherwise intimidating a person

Remember that no matter what your opinion, take any reports of bullying seriously. And seek to understand what might be considered bullying by everyone in your organization. Humor amongst old friends, especially males, can be seen as extremely aggressive out of context.

Remember that people can't read minds. Intentions don't matter as much as perception.

You may ask, what is not considered bullying? That can be even harder to answer. Many studies acknowledge there is a fine line between many behaviors and bullying. Innocent comments, tame jokes, or even seemingly benign behaviors can be perceived as bullying. A six-foot-four man that talks loudly and likes to lean in when he speaks could easily make a smaller female feel bullied. In this case, it would be easy to explain to the male how to alter his behavior, and the female could also get to know the male and determine if there is intimidation happening.

Bullying rarely includes:

- Reasonable and lawful functions
- Evaluating work performance
- Changing assignments and duties
- Delivering instructions
- Disciplinary actions when merited and within reason
- Having differing opinions
- Health and safety measures
- Workplace inspections
- Giving feedback and guidance
- Offering advice about work-related topics
- Scheduling and assigning workloads

Basically, anything that is done with reason and without malice—while being legal, moral, and ethical—is generally not considered to be bullying. Readers are always cautioned to consult with your legal counsel as definitions, rules, and policies are constantly in flux.

How bullying might affect the individual

Knowing how people react to bullying and intimidation can help you spot potential situations early. By asking a few questions in the right context, you are more likely to expose and effectively deal with a situation.

Reactions can include:

- Uncharacteristic anger
- Signs of tension and discomfort around certain individuals
- Appearing frustrated, expressing helplessness
- Having persistent or frequent headaches
- Trouble concentrating on work
- Looking tired or overly sleepy
- A perceived sense of vulnerability
- Little or no appetite
- Apparent loss of confidence
- Decreased productivity
- Expressing anxiety, panicking more easily
- Complaining of stomach pain

These reactions are usually an indicator only if they are uncharacteristic. Any noticeable deviation from normal behaviors is an indicator too.

Bullying can also affect the workplace in many ways. Even if the bullying is limited to one individual harassing another, how the situation is handled can affect the entire overall organization.

These results can include:

- Increased absence
- Increased staff turnover
- Increased anxiety and tension
- Increased costs
- Increased negative incidents
- Decreased productivity

- Decreased motivation
- Decreased morale
- Decrease in customer service

What should you do if you feel you are being bullied? If you notice you are being discriminated against or victimized in some way, you should do the following. Start by calmly and clearly explaining to the person that their behavior is not acceptable. Ask them to stop.

If you are uncomfortable, have a person you trust with you, such as a coworker, manager, or supervisor. Be sure you keep a record of all events and incidents. Record the date, the time, and a description of what happened. Include details, such as the names of people that were present or witnessed the event. Include what was said by all parties. You are recording all these incidents because the frequency and pattern will also reveal their intent. Keep copies of all emails, letters, notes, and communications you received from the person. Take pictures of everything, and save any objects no matter how awful they might be unless they are illegal or dangerous. And call the police if you need to.

Make continuous and consistent reports to your managers. Don't let them say they didn't know there was a problem. If you don't tell anyone about the situation, no one will know.

What should you **not** do if you find yourself in a situation where you think you are being bullied? First, do not strike back. It might be hard not to react, but you could easily end up looking like the bad guy. Some adept bullies count on this reaction and might be setting you up, goading you into a situation where you get in trouble for your actions.

If you are the manager or supervisor, it is important that you are committed to a program that effectively deals with this issue. An effective program to monitor and deal with should workplace bullying should do the following.

- Pertain to everyone—management, employees, vendors. clients, contractors, and anyone with a relationship with the company

- Ensure there will be no reprisals against anyone who reports an incident or experience
- Should be developed by both management and employees
- Clearly define what workplace bullying, harassment, and violence is in clear and detailed language
- Detail how reported information is handled and to whom it is disseminated
- Encourage the reporting of any incidents that are even just uncomfortable
- Guarantee the confidentiality of all parties throughout and after the process
- Be committed to fulfilling the needs of all levels of the organization
- Be dedicated to effective education and training of all the issues, policies, and procedures involved
- Consistently monitor the applicable policies
- Commit to providing support to victims at all stages of the process
- Detail the process by which people will remain anonymous. This includes witnesses and other parties involved
- Define procedures for investigating and resolving any complaints
- Develop preventive measures, implement and explain them
- Be very specific about the consequences of bullying and harassing others
- Educate people with understandable examples of the behavior you are making policies against
- Be in compliance with any local, state, federal, or international laws that may affect your workers and your organization
- Craft a clear statement of what the organization's views are on workplace bullying, what the commitment will be, and make sure everyone complies starting at the top

Tips for the workplace:

- Educate everyone about bullying. Make sure they understand that it is a serious matter.
- Let everyone know where they can go for assistance.
- Encourage everyone to act respectfully and professionally to everyone else.
- Implement a policy that includes a system of safe reporting.
- Bring in an impartial third party to help with any conflict resolutions
- Train managers to properly deal with complaints, identify any potential situations, and address situations promptly even if no complaint is filed.
- Take all complaints seriously, no matter what. Do not judge them. Deal with them quickly and confidentially.
- Attempt solutions before the situation escalates.

CHAPTER FOUR

Growth Mindset Versus Fixed Mindset

"Exceptional people seem to have a special talent for converting life's setbacks into future successes."

—Carol S. Dweck, PhD

GROWTH AND LEARNING SHOULD BE LIFELONG endeavors, and you don't need to limit yourself to one narrow avenue of learning. Likewise, personal development should be a never-ending quest. I can't emphasize enough the importance that a growth mindset plays in the success of individuals and organizations.

Conversely, a predominately fixed mindset can hold you back. I am fortunate that I have a growth mindset. The good news is that you can develop a growth mindset; you can change the way you think. Developing a growth mindset will make things in your life go so much smoother. I'm not saying it's easy to make the change, but the results make the struggle worthwhile.

I should also clarify that this discussion is predicated on common sense and wisdom. Mindsets shouldn't be black and white. Trying to change everything all the time can be just as unproductive and stifling as never considering change of any kind. You need to exercise discernment and establish boundaries to be productive. And there's safety to consider.

It is a fixed fact that humans cannot fly. No matter how hard you flap your arms, if you jump off a tall building, things won't end with you soaring into the sunset. A growth mindset would accept the fixed fact that humans cannot fly. There are a few areas where a fixed mindset is beneficial: acceptance of fixed individual traits, such as race, sexual orientation, or height. Individuals who accept themselves tend to be far better adjusted than those that don't.

A person with a growth mindset believes that people and things can change, whereas a fixed mindset believes things are unchangeable. If you believe that aspects of yourself, such as intelligence, creativity, income, and position in life, are unchangeable, you have a fixed mindset. Let's look at this closer.

While our mindsets are formed at an early age, we can change them. For example, our view of success and failure might be one way now, but we can change them. Realizing that your mistakes don't define you, building up your resiliency, learning to take on challenges, and cultivating a sense of gratitude do take work, but as I said, it is well worth the effort.

Your growth is not limited by where you started. You can change.

I slowly developed an understanding of what a growth mindset is, but a Stanford psychologist, Carol Dweck, wrote a book, *Mindset: The New Psychology of Success,* that lays it all out succinctly. She examines the power of belief, both conscious and unconscious, and explains that we can dramatically change our lives if we can change our beliefs, even a tiny bit. I know this to be true.

Dweck looked at many cultures and situations over a long period of time and proved that you can become smarter and perform better. This isn't just a self-help, positive thinking book; it's backed up by scientific research. While it does help a little to have positive self-talk, this book isn't just another tome filled with cheers and speeches. Dweck approached the subject as a professional and an accomplished academic. She discusses in detail how you can become more positive. She starts by dividing people into two groups: people with a fixed mindset and people with a growth mindset.

As I said earlier, people with a fixed mindset see intelligence as static. You're born smart or not-so-smart. This outlook is modeled by parents and is reinforced in their children. It's not always delivered in a negative message like, "You aren't that bright." The fixed mindset is also reinforced by messages like, "You are the smartest kid in your class." Parents mean well, but most kids take that message to mean that they need always be perceived as the smartest kid in the class. This message implies that not looking like the dumbest kid in class is just as important.

These messages discourage children from taking on challenges and facing obstacles with a sense of excitement. They tend to avoid any situation where they might look dumb. Even second place is unacceptable for the smartest kid in class. Fixed mindsets would rather talk about what they could do if they chose to rather than actually doing anything. They know that if they avoid a contest, they can't lose it.

Fortunately, you can choose which one you want to be.

Motivational speaker Jim Rohn said, "You are the average of the five people you spend the most time with." But before that, our wizened elders would say, "You are the company you keep." This concept is not only true in my experience, but I've also discovered there has been some significant credible research done on the concept.

Nicholas Christakis and James Fowler examined data from The Framingham Heart Study. They realized they could use this comprehensive data not only to study medical conditions but to build networks of influence between the family and friends of the participants. The data was so comprehensive that they could calculate network effects—if your close friend gains a lot of weight, there is a 45 percent chance you will too.[8]

This is so telling.

Now apply that statistic to any number of positive and negative outcomes and consider carefully who you want to spend your time with. Keep in mind that this also pertains to the positive. If you associate with positive, happy individuals with a growth mindset, you will also become more of those things. Ask yourself, which would you rather be? It's a no-brainer.

I am now a mentor and a coach and strive to continue to be of service to the business world. When I started on this path, I had nearly forty years of business experience. I could have just hung out my shingle like so many others in my shoes have, but I knew there was more to being a professional coach than just having experience. So, I attended the University of Texas at Dallas to get my executive and professional coaching certificate, and I'm glad I did.

I learned there are many skills and techniques involved in professional coaching and was excited to learn them. On the one hand, I am proud of one of my more recent business accomplishments: my team and I took the US wound care business at Mölnlycke Health Care from $28 million company to over $200 million in annual sales in eight years. I have been part of major successes at other organizations as well, yet I was humble enough to go back to school and learn. That's the growth mindset in action.

But it's not all on me. My wife, Nancy, keeps me humble. She's important in keeping me grounded. There are other people in my life that keep me grounded because I let them. I encourage them. I grow and improve as a result. If I snapped at them, argued, or ignored them, they'd stop giving me their feedback, and I'd stagnate. The people you surround yourself with play a critical

[8] Nicholas Christakis and James Fowler, "Dynamic spread of happiness in a large social network: longitudinal analysis over 20 years in the Framingham Heart Study," *BMJ* 337 (December 2008).

role in whether you stay humble. Others with a growth mindset will be comfortable telling you like it is but will not make you feel discouraged or like a failure.

When I was at Mölnlycke, my team and I completely re-engineered the culture. We created a world-class training organization in a small medical device company. I would have put our training programs up against the largest medical device companies such as Johnson & Johnson, Abbott, or 3M. It wasn't easy and took a long time, but the benefits were remarkable. We did it with what I called my five signature initiatives. We took Dweck's research to heart and transformed our organization.

We trained our people like crazy; we coached them, mentored them, and put very attractive incentive plans in place. Everybody rallied behind the cause. It took some time to get rolling, but there was no stopping us once momentum took hold.

One program we initiated toward the end of my career at Mölnlycke was game-changing. We gathered all 150 women in the US organization—not just the leaders or the high potential employees—and flew them to the Dallas Fort Worth airport for a two-day program that discussed the challenges and opportunities of being women in the workforce. I brought in a key group of marquee women speakers from all over the United States. We had an unbelievable response to that program. We had so many women step up and say they wanted to move up; they wanted to develop and get into management positions. They demonstrated a growth mindset, and we helped them grow. The program's cost was more than offset by the savings we realized by not having to go through recruiters to hire talent outside the organization.

The growth mindset combines unbridled confidence and deep humility. One person I've met over my life that embodies this more than most is Anne Welsh McNulty.

I met Anne as a result of participating in Stanford's Distinguished Careers Institute. Anne had an incredibly successful career from several standpoints, including financial gain. But the amazing thing about Anne is her humility. She came from a very modest background. Her mom never went to college, her dad was a WWII veteran who went to college on the GI Bill, and she was one of many children. But Anne was instilled with a growth mindset. She earned her MBA in Finance and Insurance from the Wharton School at the University of Pennsylvania. She was valedictorian of her graduating class at Villanova University and later received an honorary doctorate from Villanova. Anne was an Advanced Leadership Initiative Fellow at Harvard University in 2015 and a Distinguished Careers Institute Fellow at Stanford University in 2017.

And Anne is paying it forward. She's started The McNulty Foundation (https://mcnultyfound.org/). The mission of the foundation is the definition of the growth mindset.

> "At the John P. & Anne Welsh McNulty Foundation, we inspire, develop and drive leaders to solve the most critical challenges of our time.
>
> We believe that opportunity is a human right and that barriers to opportunity—poor education, poor basic services, poor access to markets—represent an unacceptable loss of potential. We believe that all of us want to live meaningful lives, build better ones for our children, and take ownership of our futures and their communities. We believe those who have benefitted from opportunity have an obligation to use their talents to expand opportunity and unlock the potential of others. The best leadership, we believe, creates agency in those it touches, gives them a stake in their communities, and inspires the next generation."

Are you curious about what your mindset might be? Here's a quick checklist to get you started.

A growth mindset believes:

- Intelligence can be improved
- Challenges are opportunities and not threats
- In acknowledging weaknesses and does not deny them

- Peer pressure has no significant influence
- Their goals are achievable
- In perseverance rather than giving up easily
- Hard work is more important than innate talents
- Hard work is not speculative; it always pays off
- You have much control over your destiny; you're not a victim of eternal forces
- A new experience is exciting, not scary

The results of a fixed mindset are evident when you know what to look for. A person's view of themself profoundly affects every aspect of their life. It actually makes good sense when you understand the underpinnings.

We see people all the time that are intent on constantly proving themselves. They are the people that one-up you in every conversation, name drop, and mention their accomplishments *ad nauseam*. Since they view the world as a contest, they always play to win the prize of looking the best, the smartest, and the most successful.

Every conversation, every situation, is evaluated through this lens. They ask themselves questions like, "Will I look smart if I do this or dumb if I fail? Can I make sure I look the best? If not, how can the shame of being less than perfect be deflected away from me? If I buy this item, will those who see me think I am better than they are?"

In the growth mindset, situations are viewed differently. People with this mindset are concerned about learning, growing, helping, and generally more positive and inclusive outcomes.

Do not mistake the growth mindset as a Pollyanna view of the world. The point isn't that you can be absolutely anything you want to become with the right mindset. A growth mindset simply means that a person has the potential to be far greater than they are in the present. A growth mindset is a knowledge that years of passion and hard work will result in great rewards—whatever they may be.

You have to ask yourself do you want to become better or waste time trying to prove you are better than you actually are? Do you want to exert your efforts trying to hide your flaws or seek to overcome them? Do you want friends who like a person that doesn't exist or ones that will appreciate you and help you grow?

*

When you understand the growth mindset, you will see how things operate—how beliefs you might have assumed were carved in stone, when changed, can lead to an avalanche of new thoughts and actions that will change the trajectory of your life for the better.

Growth Mindset Exercises

If you do not possess a natural inclination toward a growth mindset, you can change if you want to. Here are a few pointers and exercises that can help.

I'm committed.

Being committed is one of the most important things you can do. This means when things get hard, you keep trying. It might be your habit to quit when things get complicated; you might have a fixed mindset, inner-self-talk well-rehearsed and ready to talk you out of any challenge. But you need to tune it out as you rewire your brain, change your habits, and give yourself an entirely new script for your inner-self-talk. Remember, you are taking on a challenge to achieve and accomplish, not get credit or accolades.

Bring it on.

New challenges can make you feel vulnerable, confused, overwhelmed, and as if everyone is looking at you askance. It is a feeling many of us will never get used to. Let people look because those with a fixed mindset don't matter, and those with a growth mindset will cheer you on and attempt to help you. When you do conquer whatever challenge you have faced, you will be rewarded with the sense of accomplishment, how awesome it feels, and it will get much easier each time to let yourself be uncomfortable. You might find that you start to crave that feeling because you know that it is but a precursor to a win.

I'm never too old.

Age is no excuse. A growth mindset doesn't factor age into the equation. You are never too old to learn something new. Say you are fifty years old and considering some training for a change in careers. One way to look at it is you are too old, people will think you are foolish, or you will be dead soon. Or you can think about the fact that you don't know when you will die. You can spend the remainder of your life engaged, active, and really living. Or you can fade away. You can let your cognitive abilities decline as they atrophy.

I can always get better.

Our discussion about failure brings up another point. What is success? If you think that success means you can never get better at something because you don't need to, you will not be as successful as you could be. Look at how often world-class Olympic athletes compete only to better their own world records. You don't think of most things in terms of winning or losing or being better than so-and-so; you seek to beat yourself. You are focused on improving, learning, and doing better than yourself. Read the story of many successful persons, and you will often find a vast record of what you might call failures.

How can I get better?

A big part of getting better is a humble and honest look at yourself and your performance. You are honest with yourself about your effort and attitude. You don't make excuses; you take ownership and create solutions.

Self-analysis can be tough when you have a defensive, fixed mindset. But objectively owning up to your shortcomings, missteps, and plain old terrible choices is a huge step toward real progress.

Success is my guidepost.

Successful people often have histories of failures. False starts, failed businesses, unpublished books, box office bombs—you name it, very successful people have failed more times than unsuccessful people because they kept trying.

When you stop looking at status symbols and price tags as markers of success, you will see that the signpost of real success is the number of times a person has tried again, not how many times they have won. A growth mindset sees the success of others as something that was earned, something to be celebrated, and an opportunity to learn more about becoming successful.

Determination determines success.

Having the desire, passion, and unstoppable drive to do something is what makes successful people successful. It has been said that successful people do the things that unsuccessful people do not do. Remaining focused on the big goal despite any setbacks keeps successful people moving forward. They just learn, adjust, and keep going.

I am always learning.

A person with a fixed mindset always tries to prove what they know or point out what others don't know. A growth mindset wants to learn. They know that they don't know everything and will ask questions, seek answers, and listen more than they talk. They know that they will never know everything, and they are

OK with that. They are excited about the next new thing they can learn, the next new experience or activity.

I am what I am.

For good or bad, you are what you are right now. You can use that reality to support a fixed mindset and list all the reasons you can't do something, why you are a victim, or how you missed your window. Or, with a growth mindset, you can take that reality as a starting point on a journey to a better place. A growth mindset knows that everyone has advantages and disadvantages. Everyone has challenges, some are very obvious (like a physical handicap), and some are unseen (such as a mental condition, domestic abuse, addictions, and more). The fact is, we never know what people are struggling with, so we can't assume that everyone has it made and we are the only ones with a problem.

I don't seek the approval of others.

A growth mindset is not externally motivated by the opinions of others. A growth mindset is motivated by passion and mission, all internal for the most part. Improving is for your benefit, not so others will admire you. Detaching yourself from needing the approval of others gives you the freedom to focus on what you really want and to pursue it.

Good enough isn't.

A growth mindset looks to models of success as their guides. We move in the direction of where we look, so they move upward. However, a fixed mindset looks at their feet as they explain why their mediocre work is good enough, why they were late (because so-and-so was too), and a long list of "yeah, buts" and "if only." They, of course, move downward.

Growth mindsets can be obsessive about getting things right. They back off and ask themselves questions like, "Have I given this my best effort?" "Can I do better?" They don't blame the tools; they use them. A growth mindset believes that if one person can do something, so can many others. A growth mindset knows that with belief and hard work, you can eventually learn anything. They are realistic and know that while they might have limits, they are diligent about removing any self-imposed limit. They tackle so-called accepted limits. Then they challenge and push those limits.

*

Growth and learning should be lifelong pursuits. Personal development should be a never-ending quest, and a growth mindset is critical to the success of individuals and organizations. Developing a growth mindset will make things in your life go so much smoother. I'm not saying it's easy to make the change, but the results make the struggle well worth the effort. And common sense and wisdom should be used when seeking to exceed your limits.

CHAPTER FIVE

Self-Awareness

> "Self-awareness is the most difficult task any of us faces. But until you know yourself, strengths and weaknesses, you cannot succeed in any but the most superficial sense of the word."
>
> —Warren Bennis

THE IMPORTANCE OF SELF-AWARENESS IN LEADERSHIP and management cannot be overstated. We can start with an examination of our own biases. This alone is a daunting task that requires one to be authentic, vulnerable, and humble. The first step is to understand that you have biases.

The word bias is defined as a prejudice in favor of or against one thing, person, or group compared with another, usually in a way considered to be unfair. We all have biases based on where, when, and how we were raised, among many other factors. Being aware of the perspective from which you operate, your worldview as formed based on your upbringing and experiences will make you a far better leader.

While it is impossible to be fully aware of all your biases, it is important to try, especially in the realm of management and leadership. You most likely won't view the world the same as the people you oversee, which can create issues that range from simple miscommunication to possibly offending someone.

Behavioral scientists believe that bias is a survival mechanism that evolved from the need to make a split-second, life-and-death decision. Our brains have evolved over a long period to make these snap decisions, but our civilization has evolved much faster. We no longer need to—and shouldn't—make decisions in such a mindless fashion. One of the best tools for dealing with bias is to slow down and question your decisions. Take the time to be sure that you are not making a decision based on race, gender, etc. Then remove those factors from your decision-making.

Expanding on our pursuit of self-awareness, let's look at our concept of self.

I teach marketing as an adjunct instructor at the School of Business at Texas Wesleyan University. In our course textbook, *Contemporary Marketing (17th ed.)* by Boone and Curves, the chapter on consumer behavior discusses Self-Theory, the notion that a person's self-concept is made up of four components. Self-Theory directly addresses self-awareness. The theory looks at the perception of the individual from four points of view: self-image, ideal-self, looking-glass-self, and real-self.

Let's look at those more closely.

- **Self-Image** is what we think about ourselves. It is the beliefs that have formed our identity over our life, mostly unconsciously.
- **Ideal-Self** is the way we would like to be. The ideal-self motivates us to do things we think will create our ideal-self.
- **Looking-Glass-Self** is our perception of how others perceive us compared to how we see ourselves.
- **Real-Self** is what others show you relating to your self-image. When others interact with us, we get feedback on our perception of our self. We use that feedback to adjust our self-image accordingly.

In our endeavor to become more self-aware, these concepts can help us understand why we think the way we do, making it easier to refine our thinking. Looking at Self-Theory as explained above, we can see how using a celebrity in a marketing campaign can be effective. Many people are convinced that if they use Aveeno, their skin will look as good as Jennifer Aniston's skin, the actress in the Aveeno commercials.

When faced with certain situations, understanding how you think can be very important. When you are managing under ideal circumstances, things are calm, and you have time to consider options, it's easy. But when things get crazy and you need to act quickly, the amount of work you've put into your self-awareness can really pay off. I was once literally in a life-and-death situation and was grateful for past training I'd received.

One morning at work, I got a call from an employee. She had been going through an exceedingly difficult personal challenge and told me she just couldn't take it anymore. She was distraught and sounded suicidal. I immediately connected her with a crisis counselor through our company's employee assistance program. I knew better than to try to handle this myself. I also had her parents' phone number; fortunately, they lived nearby and were able to get to her house quickly.

I was grateful that I had training as both a health advocate and a companion (peer counselor) when I was an undergraduate at the University of Southern California. I had never used this training, but I was so glad I had it that day. It kept me calm. I knew to get a qualified professional to help her immediately.

It was an awful situation, but I was glad she felt comfortable enough to call me. That made a huge difference in the outcome of the situation. Instead of the tragedy that could have unfolded, she worked through her extraordinarily challenging situation and was back to being a wonderful, fun-loving person.

It's all about training. It was my training that kept me calm and helped me make the right decisions. The inclination is to help a person in distress, for most decent people, but the best help you can sometimes give a person is calling in a professional and stepping back.

On that note, there will be times and situations where you simply cannot go it alone. Everyone needs help occasionally, and you should be able to ask for it when needed. People have weaknesses, shortcomings, and flaws. I have my own and plenty of them.

When I was in elementary school, the principal would come on the PA system every day during the lunch recess and summon the kids that had been acting up to his office. It was not uncommon to hear my name called. I'd go to the office and sit on a small, hard bench. I was probably in trouble for pushing people or acting up in some way. I just couldn't sit still. It was so active in class that once, in fourth grade, my teacher sent me outside to run laps around the track. She forgot about me for almost an hour. When she came out, I was still running. For me running around that track was pure bliss.

It was suggested that I take Ritalin. However, my mom didn't think it was the right thing to do, so she refused. In hindsight, I probably should have been medicated. In any case, I worked hard and learned how to study and cope with my ADHD. But I have still not ever conquered it completely. I was most fortunate to be in a school that understood my situation and helped me advance despite my challenges.

I accepted and faced my condition. I didn't let it define me. I didn't feel broken or flawed; it was simply something I had to deal with. I wonder if having to manage my ADHD is what made me a successful manager. Having such a struggle certainly gave me empathy for those who struggled in silence with a challenge.

A new national survey, "Capturing America's Attention," indicates adults with ADHD have lifelong impairments that severely affect many areas of their lives, including educational and professional achievement, self-image, relationships, substance abuse, and virtually every aspect of their life. This is the first survey to examine the impacts ADHD has on adults, and it is grim. It is estimated that 4 percent of US adults are affected by ADHD, and it is often attributed to preventing adults from reaching their full potential. The effects that stem from the condition and its effects are damaging to self-esteem, relationships, and their overall outlook on life. Frustration with the condition often drives people to harmful behaviors such as self-medication and acting out in self-destructive ways. My ADHD could have derailed me; adults with ADHD are three times more likely to suffer from stress, depression, and other emotional problems. Yet, I believe that my ability to be self-aware saved me, at least in this case.

There is the notion that people with ADHD can lose a lot of time by not being fully engaged with the world around them, and I've noticed that happening to me. But fortunately, in my case, I did learn to deal with it. It was only by being self-aware and honest that I could develop the strategies to deal with something that had the potential to sink me. One of those strategies was to ask for help when I needed it.

I told my staff to stop me if I went off on a tangent at my last job. They were comfortable calling me out, and I was glad for it. When you have ADHD, the smallest thing can distract you and send you way off course—a word, a sound, anything. If you aren't aware of it or take measures to help with your lack of awareness, you will follow that path no matter where it goes, how long it takes you off course, or how insignificant or unrelated it might be.

You have to be transparent with people, not only about yourself but about them as well. A person needs to know what skills and competencies you're looking for and what you believe their skills and competencies are. They need to know what they need to do to bridge any gaps they have. Whether it's something the company can help with or something they need to do on their own, we all need to work together.

It's also important that multiple people be involved in any major decision. The hiring process, for example, should include more than just the team in human resources. The people who have to rely on a potential new hire, manage them, and work alongside them should all have a chance to chime in. This is vitally important today as companies are matrixed and project-oriented, and much of the work involves cross-functional, company-wide projects. This is another area where managers tend to overstep when they form and operate on one opinion and don't seek the opinions and assessments of those directly or indirectly affected.

Speaking of others, you need to be self-aware when around other people, no matter what the setting.

At one sales conference, a woman was very proud of some work she'd had done on herself recently. One thing led to another, and soon she had a group of men up in her room getting a show of the work. One of the men felt pressured to go up to the room to participate and afterward filed an informal complaint against the woman. He felt like he'd been harassed into participating from the pressure of the other men in the group.

It was a development opportunity for everyone involved. This incident drove home the point for me that you've got to always be self-aware at all times, particularly when you're at a company event.

No matter how self-aware we can become, some traits are can be very challenging to change. That isn't always bad. With an open mind and a growth mindset, you can develop strategies for your weaknesses, even turning them into strengths. Let's look at neurotic behavior.

Like many other things, neuroticism will likely become a problem if denied or left unmanaged. However, if dealt with openly and honestly, you stand a far better chance of success. Daniel Nettle wrote the book *Personality: What makes you the way you are.* In the book, he explains that neurotic people often have an inner self-directed drive to succeed. Their tendency toward rumination is often wrapped up in neuroses, but it can be an asset if your job requires being detail-oriented.

Neuroticism is our ability to adjust to psychological distress. A neurotic obsesses over a negative experience. Rather than easily adjusting to events, neurotics cannot adapt quickly when leadership requires it and will dwell on the negative. They don't cope well with stress, which leaders must do daily.

Everyone has some amount of neuroticism, but leaders need to have less of it. Leaders must be able to face stress without becoming upset or rattled. Clearly, some situations will evoke unavoidable stress responses created to protect us.

Fortunately, our personality traits can be appreciated, managed, developed, and modified as needed as we strive to be effective leaders.

Let's look at the five-factor model of personality (FFM) developed by Robert McCrae and Paul Costa.[9] FFM is a helpful tool in the pursuit of self-awareness. It can create a simple blueprint of your and others' behavior. You can remember the five factors with the acronym OCEAN.

1. Openness to experience means you like to try new things and prefer variety. The opposite would be to prefer a routine and stay in your comfort zone.
2. Conscientiousness means you plan ahead, get things done quickly, and are detail-oriented. The opposite would be a spontaneous approach to work, loose with schedules, messy, and prone to procrastination.
3. Extroversion means you are a conversation starter, have a large social group, and are energized by socializing. The opposite would be a preference for solitude, a person who finds socializing exhausting and dislikes small talk.
4. Agreeableness means you play well with others, have a tendency toward cooperation, helpfulness, and compassion. The opposite is to be generally disagreeable and unfeeling.
5. Neuroticism generally refers to your level of anxiety. On one end of the scale, a person can remain calm under pressure, while on the other, there's incapacitating worry and fear.

---

[9] Robert McCrae and Paul Costa, "The Five-Factor Model and the NEO Inventories," *Oxford handbook of personality assessment,* (Oxford: Oxford University Press) 299–322.

Where do you fall on the high to low spectrum for each of these five traits? This simple exercise will help you understand your own personality better. With that information, you can be a more informed and aware leader as you will be able to construct an environment that works for you and your team. In addition, you can better understand others through observation and discussion based on the five traits.

In addition to all that we've discussed here, there are many other ways you can increase your self-awareness. Warren Bennis said that an effective leader is one who constantly seeks to improve themselves. Improvement can be made in many ways, such as seeking a mentor, reading, peer discussion—the list is almost endless.

You don't need to keep your quest for improvement focused within your industry. You can learn from other sources and people. There are myriad resources beyond this book to help you in your quest to become a better leader. In my experience, the best leaders are those who are highly self-aware and constantly developing and improving.

*

I leave you with these four lessons for self-knowledge from *On Becoming a Leader* by Warren Bennis.[10]

- One: You are your own best teacher.
- Two: Accept responsibility. Blame no one.
- Three: You can learn anything you want to learn.
- Four: True understanding comes from reflecting on your experience.

All those things are important to maintaining an understanding of self-awareness.

---

[10] Warren G. Bennis, *On Becoming a Leader*, (New York, New York: Basic Books, 2009).

CHAPTER SIX

Hypocritical Leadership

"What you do has a far greater impact than what you say."

—Stephen Covey

As we saw in the previous chapter, being aware of hypocrisy is part of self-awareness. Hypocrisy deserves a chapter of its own. Hypocrisy by those in leadership positions is toxic and has many forms.

You probably know what hypocrisy is—it's to expect others to conform to standards or rules to which you do not conform. While it can be challenging to keep our words and actions aligned as leaders, we must be acutely aware of the consistency of our words and deeds. People notice what leaders do and say, but they are also very sensitive to the reality of the behaviors and messages compared to the narrative coming from the top as well as managers within the organization.

While most materials on hypocrisy focus on the simple definition of hypocrisy, I would like to break it out in more subtle detail to look at a range of what could be considered hypocritical behavior. In *Hypocrisy and Moral Seriousness (1994),* Roger Crisp and Christopher Cowton proposed four forms of hypocrisy that exist in the self and others: inconsistency, pretense, blame, and complacency.[11]

Inconsistency is to say one thing and do another or the "practice what you preach" model. For example, a manager who tells his employees to look sharp but doesn't shave and wears wrinkled clothing fits this model. Or the preacher who preaches the ten commandments and the dire consequences of not abiding by them but routinely breaks them. We start here because Crisp and Cowton realize this is the base, most simple form of hypocrisy and is usually considered a complete definition by most, but there are distinctions.

Pretense is explained as a trick or deception. When an individual works to perfect a public image in opposition to their true nature, that is pretense. It goes both ways, but generally, the genuinely good person that feigns being bad—like the persona of a rock star—isn't frowned upon as much. People who practice pretense are attempting to elevate themselves above others with their efforts, whereas people who blame others are doing the opposite.

Blame is the hypocrisy of criticizing a person for a fault you possess—the boss who criticizes his employees for being lazy while demonstrating the same behavior. Blame can almost be comical to witness, if not so infuriating, especially if you are the one in the crosshairs. The phrase "the pot calling the kettle black" comes to mind.

Blamers are experts at sidestepping any attempt to point out their hypocrisy with various reasons and justifications for why "It's different when I do it." Instead, blamers tend to go on the offensive and achieve their superior position by taking down the

[11] Roger Crisp and Christopher Cowton, "Hypocrisy and Moral Seriousness," *American Philosophical Quarterly* 31, no. 4 (1994): 343-49.

other party. As mentioned earlier, blamers are the opposite of those engaged in pretense in their approach.

Complacency is unaware or uninformed self-satisfaction. Technicalities and loopholes or convenient logic serve this person well. The complacent do the minimum required to give the impression that they are what they want to appear to be.

Complacency and pretense are similar, but there is a distinction. The pretentious hypocrite pretends they believe what they preach, but the complacent hypocrite may believe what they claim but are too weak or lazy to put it into practice.

Why is this topic so critical to management? Because leaders are largely responsible for establishing an organization's ethics, the leaders' own ethics are paramount. To function successfully, an organization must operate from an ethical basis. When a leader demonstrates unethical behavior, such as hypocrisy, the organization's culture is negatively impacted and can become toxic. Conversely, when a leader performs actions consistent with what they say, their followers are more likely to follow suit and work congruently.

When employees can count on others to help them because they have been helpful previously, organizations thrive. Once hypocrisy becomes prevalent, trust is lost within the organization. Long-term visions break down. Employees begin to think only of themselves rather than the good of the group. Once the group breaks down, there's no mutual trust; it's every person for themselves. Without long-term thinking, a company is doomed, especially in today's rapidly changing environment.

One of the most crippling results of this breakdown occurs when employees are compelled to do only the minimal amount of work required to get by. At this point, the company's long-term interests take a back seat, and ultimately people start looking for a way out of the toxic environment. As a result, people leave. Unfortunately, it is often the best people that leave first because they can, and it becomes increasingly harder to replace and retain employees.

Working for a person that practices hypocritical leadership is extremely uncomfortable, difficult, and frustrating. I once worked with a very prominent executive who operated his business by a set of rules he didn't follow. One such example was that a person must be in a job position for a certain amount of time before being promoted. Another rule was that employees were required to have a college degree. He was exempt from his own rules, and people noticed. It had a negative impact on the entire organization.

Had he addressed some of the seemingly hypocritical choices openly, it would have gone a long way to appeasing those below him who had to abide by a different set of rules. However, there is a difference between hypocrisy, which is a present action, and following a set of rules forged in past experiences and wisdom. Like a parent, just because a leader has made mistakes in the past doesn't give employees the license to make those same mistakes.

If this executive had explained the policy, he might not have seemed hypocritical. Maybe the rule about degrees changed due to growth. Since the advent of the internet, the number of applications companies receive has increased a thousand-fold. It makes sense that a company might need to par down the number of applications received to make things manageable for HR. Maybe there is a rule that the CEO can approve a nondegree hire as many outstanding people didn't go to college.

But if the stated rule is that you must have a degree to work at the company and it is enforced arbitrarily, that's hypocritical. This situation is demoralizing and frustrating to those affected negatively and an example of poor behavior for those affected positively.

A fairly and consistently enforced rule need not apply to everyone across the board. There's nothing wrong with a CEO requiring everyone have a college degree even if they don't have one. But if the top-performing people at the company did not graduate from college, it makes sense to have an exception to the rule. Job descriptions often state a degree requirement with the addendum or X number of years of equivalent experience.

But this particular CEO wasn't consistent, and his hypocritical leadership was damaging. He routinely violated his own stated rules and leapfrogged certain people up the corporate ladder, leaving others wondering what had happened. "I was told no, and now so-and-so is jumping up the ladder." It is understandable why that would be very frustrating.

Part of the problem is that leaders and upper management rarely feel obligated to explain themselves. "I'm your boss, do your job." They don't feel required to justify or explain themselves to a subordinate. They don't see how their behavior is demotivating their people, and they blame the employees rather than themselves. People get beaten down bit by bit; the trust they have in the leader drops. The hopes they have for their career erodes as they adopt the attitude of "why try?" They can no longer count on their leader to speak truthfully. What will the next exception to a rule be? How will it deprive those affected out of a promotion, an opportunity, or even a job?

Leaders and managers are very visible, particularly in large organizations, so their actions significantly impact the organization. Sometimes they even have a massive public impact—for example, the behavior of many politicians during this pandemic.

Numerous examples of public figures preached the importance of masks, social distancing, and even sought to pass laws to enforce these suggestions that immediately demonstrated highly public acts of hypocrisy. Some politicians flew to visit family right after a press conference urging everyone to stay safe and stay home. Others actively banned indoor dining, only to proceed directly to a restaurant immediately after the session. While people were scared to go to the grocery, living in lockdown, and struggling financially, they saw the very people that put them in the situation doing the exact opposite. In the internet age, these examples went viral immediately. It's insulting and confusing. Worst still, this behavior undermines the message and leaves people wondering if they need to follow any precautions at all.

An effective leader earns respect and trust, and trust is critical for any organization to thrive. An effective leader talks the talk and walks the walk.

When management is sincere and functions as part of an organization and not above it, they inspire loyalty and model excellence. When management is accessible and available, employees feel respected and vital to the organization. It can be highly motivating when a manager rolls up their sleeves to assist or understand the employees they manage.

It's a fact that engaged executives, those that get their hands dirty and demonstrate leadership, are far more effective. For example, Lars-Johan Jarnheimer, former CEO of Tele2 AB, a Swedish-based telecommunications firm, increased revenue by over 500 percent because of his personal involvement with customers. He worked in the call center a few days a year to demonstrate just how important the customers are. Bezos, the founder and executive chairman of Amazon, does this and similar activities, as well.

How to spot a hypocrite

Sonnenberg created a list of twenty-three ways to spot a hypocrite.[12] I found many of his items very similar, so I selected my top ten.

Hypocrites:

1. Say one thing but do another
2. Treat those in power differently than they do underlings
3. Preach tolerance but judge others who don't conform to their way of thinking
4. Volunteer others but rarely raise their hand
5. Say one thing to someone's face but another behind their back

12 Frank Sonnenberg, "23 Ways to Spot a Hypocrite," *Frank Sonnenberg Online*, November 5, 2019, https://www.franksonnenbergonline.com/blog/23-ways-to-spot-a-hypocrite/.

6. Pretend to be wealthy even though their bank account is bare
7. Help people only when it's in their personal interest to do so
8. Demand austerity for others but handsomely compensate themselves
9. Feign outrage even though they have no intention of doing anything about it
10. Judge others but call people intolerant when they're personally judged

*

We need to root hypocrisy out of our organizations, but there will always be exceptions to the rules. The employee of the month may be the only person allowed to park in a special space. Or only salespeople that have achieved X sales goal can use the company condo. Exceptions are fine, but these differences can be perceived as hypocrisy when not properly communicated.

Management will do what they need to do for the business; they will make exceptions to the rules. What's important is that the reasons for these actions need to be clarified to everyone.

Lead openly and honestly as the *appearance* of hypocrisy can be as damaging as being hypocritical.

CHAPTER SEVEN

Micromanagement And Design By Committee

"It doesn't make sense to hire smart people and then tell them what to do; we hire smart people and they tell us what to do."

—Steve Jobs

"To err is human, but to really screw things up requires a design committee of bureaucrats."

—Henry Spencer

THIS CHAPTER COMBINES TWO EXTREMES OF management that are equally stifling: micromanaging and design by committee. In one extreme, a single person tells everyone what to do; in the other, everyone tells one person what to do.

It seems logical that neither approach will produce good results, but it is easy to fall into one of these two stifling practices. Let's look at micromanagement first. Micromanagement generally involves one person and can become a predominant practice within an organization.

Micromanagement

Some micromanaging is done with seemingly good intentions, and, in some instances, it may be necessary. However, more often than not, micromanaging happens when a manager or leader has not been properly trained and coached or cannot operate well under pressure.

Managers are not puppeteers, and employees are not puppets. An employee should be able to function with a set of instructions and minimal supervision. If a manager is over an employee's shoulder every step of the way, that is micromanaging! Occasional over-the-shoulder direction needs to happen. Still, if the manager is overly critical and domineering and ignores the expertise and abilities of the employee, that is disruptive and damaging and frankly, not productive. So why does it still happen, time and time again?

Micromanagers tend to be insecure people or insecure in their jobs. Occasionally, they may be a narcissist or might even suffer from obsessive-compulsive disorder (OCD). Individuals prone to micromanaging will tend to do so if they are up against a deadline or under a lot of pressure. And, unfortunately, sometimes micromanagement is a deliberate tactic used to make an employee quit.

Whatever its cause, the effects of micromanaging are always damaging. Teaching, training, coaching, and mentoring can at times be equally detailed and intrusive, but they are generally positive, whereas micromanaging is almost always negative.

It's difficult enough to manage a vast global organization with multiple locations, but micromanagement on this scale is a nightmare. And often, it is a needlessly concocted overreaction and blatant mismanagement.

Running a global organization can be done by centralizing your operations and running everything from headquarters or decentralizing and giving everyone a lot of autonomy. You can be anywhere on the spectrum between centralization to decentralization. There are tradeoffs with each approach, but total centralization is generally bad for a complex global operation as it tends to promote a milieu of micromanagement by headquarters.

I was once involved with a national sales meeting for a US-based division of a global company. The meeting took place in Huntington Beach, California. The meeting had a theme as most national sales meetings have. Now, I've been to at least twenty of these meetings, and I can't tell you the theme of most of them. The theme is not important; it's often used as an acute motivational tool, a sort of rallying cry for the sales team.

At this meeting, the theme was "Catch the wave." It seemed apropos for the shores of the Pacific Ocean, but some of the leaders in the global headquarters hated it. They didn't think it was appropriate for some reason. Their response was to set up a committee after the conclusion of that sales meeting to oversee all future sales meetings. One of the jobs of this committee was to determine the theme of every sales meeting worldwide. There's no way to choose a theme that will work globally and be relevant to the situation facing each country at a unique time. It was a ridiculous waste of time and money in its futility, and what's more, no one cares over the long term about a specific theme of a particular one-off sales meeting. It's difficult enough to run a global business without such nonsense serving as a distraction.

The damage caused by micromanaging can be severe. A micromanaged employee often feels that they are not trusted to do their job, and they feel disrespected. As a result, they hesitate to take the initiative to do any unsupervised work. In addition, they often will be led to believe that any work they do will never be acceptable, and they will end up redoing the work once the boss is back looking over their shoulder.

When an employee feels untrusted by management, they in turn distrust management. They know that new ideas will be ignored, shot down, and possibly even stolen. When an employee is afraid to share new ideas, and this becomes systemic, innovation may slow to a trickle or even come to a halt.

If they stick around, micromanaged employees end up needing more micromanagement. They can become totally demotivated due to the toxic environment and stressed out from the damage done to their confidence in their skills and abilities. And, by always being told what to do, the employee has learned little of value along the way. They've spent so much time and energy mastering the difficulties of working for a micromanager, they've neglected to develop and advance at the job they were hired to do.

As expected, people in this situation usually seek to escape the micromanager. They feel no loyalty to the manager or the company and start looking for a new job.

So, how do you identify micromanagement? Answer these questions as accurately and honestly as you can. Consider them from both the perspective of the boss and the employee.

Are you constantly watched or questioned about your work? First, you need to determine if you've done something to merit that treatment. If not, you might be getting micromanaged. Next, ask yourself if you are slacking off. Are you doing a poor job? Is your manager too involved in your work for a reason? How we show up to work is affected by our personal life; perhaps personal challenges are impacting our performance at work.

Do you sense that your boss or project lead is hesitant to give you assignments? Are you new and need to get up to speed? Have you messed up in the past? Or does the boss do this with everyone? Is the boss reluctant to trust anyone with a task? Do they overexplain things? Do they dole out simple tasks in small numbers, so it is easy to monitor and oversee the employees as they work?

Does your boss seek information and opinions from others based on their skills, experience, and education? Or is it a one-way relationship that involves only downward commands and dictates?

Once you know the answers to these questions, you can decide the extent to which you are micromanaging or being micromanaged. People need to be trusted to do their jobs, and bosses need to be trusted to do right by the employees. There can be updates and progress reports on a project, feedback given and received, with no micromanagement taking place.

Practice delegating and waiting to build trust. Focus on the goals of the outcome and not every step involved in getting there. Don't look at your employees as subordinates, rather as collaborators. If you listen and respect what they offer and genuinely consider it, they will feel respected and not overpowered when you engage in any back and forth with them.

Be sure that communication between you and the team is open and honest.

How do you deal with a micromanager as an employee?

Let's assume that you are being micromanaged because your boss is stressed out, worried, or just operates that way, and you aren't the reason for the extreme hands-on treatment.

First, realize that the micromanager's behavior has nothing to do with you. But the right way to handle this isn't pushing back; after all, they're your boss, and it won't end well. Instead, you have to be the one to ease the situation.

Start by assessing their behavior. Is your boss a person with high standards that treats everyone this way? Steve Jobs is a prime example. He was fanatical about details and perfection. His standards were high, and people generally knew what they were getting into when they signed up under him.

If your boss is stressed out or worried, try to clarify the tasks at hand. Ambiguity in assignments often drives managers to want to overmanage. Yes, they created this situation but try to push for clarity. Be clear on what is expected of you and when your boss will give feedback. Ask questions with respect and interest, and the boss will feel heard. Take notes. Keep an open mind that you might even learn something from this person despite his style.

Communicate—let them know what's going on at regular intervals. Give them updates so they feel they have some control of the progress of your work. You can send emails or schedule regular review or status meetings to make them feel like part of the process. They are your boss, so they should have some idea and say-so.

A little effort to manage the micromanager can save a lot of time and frustration later on.

Design by Committee

Design by committee is commonly used as a derogatory term to describe a project with too many people involved in the decision-making. As a result, there is no unified design or vision. With no key vision holder or decision-maker, this process usually produces poor results. Numerous compromises are made to the initial design requirements. Worse still, many participants often lack the skill and training to make such decisions. The process becomes overly complex, inconsistent, and often dragged out.

This term is used across numerous fields and is cited as the reason for failures of all kinds. In one case, a school in the UK created by the merging of several other schools was named by the community. The result was a twelve-word name, *The Knowsley Park Centre for Learning, Serving Prescot, Whiston, and the Wider Community*. Finally, the principal shortened it to *The Prescot School.*

Another accepted piece of common sense is that design by committee doesn't necessarily provide the best outcomes or results. Design by committee can minimize your best people and ideas with those perhaps not so capable. The results are rarely greater than the sum of the parts.

I worked for a global company that decided it was time for a new website. Quickly, the process encompassed all country websites. A huge project evolved, and it took substantially longer than it should have because there were too many people involved. Every level of the company, from upper management, legal, marketing, PR—you name it—was involved and wanted to have a say. You can't get anything done in a complex, international company with thousands of employees if everyone gets a say. Businesses aren't designed to be run like elections where everyone gets a vote.

There's were so many egos, objectives, widely varying levels of competencies, and agendas in play that it was a doomed project from the start. Who goes on the website? What order are they listed?

Do they get a picture? A bio? Do we include contact information? How should they dress? It gets political and personal. It took this company over a year to decide on a design for their website.

Everyone had a say-so. No one had ultimate responsibility and accountability.

And it didn't end at the launch of the site. During the entire time the site was being designed, there was a hold on all local market websites. No one could make changes or post updates to their local market site. With such inertia, our site became more out of date and irrelevant with each passing day.

While you must avoid design by committee, maintaining a collaborative design process is essential. Collaboration among those with requisite competencies and skills enables teams to deliver high-quality work. So how do you achieve this balance between collaboration and design by committee? First, eradicate politics, ego, and personal agendas.

A project needs a unifying vision and a well-designed decision-making process that facilitates and compels the successful design. Not everyone is qualified to give feedback; the decision-maker(s) needs to have final authority.

Mishandled feedback and unclear authority are costly in terms of time and money—and worse, morale. When you force experts to prototype and test designs they know are nonstarters from the get-go, they become demotivated, frustrated, and fatigued. You risk squandering all their excitement and enthusiasm for the project.

How do you include an organization in the planning of a product while avoiding design by committee? First, you need to develop a system and well communicated and transparent processes to manage feedback. Second, you need to manage expectations and establish guidelines from the beginning. If you don't, you will end up with a horrible mess and a worthless collage of opinions and ideas. No one will be happy about the results.

You don't want to make people feel you disregarded their feedback, and you don't want them to think they are part of the design team. Therefore, feedback needs to be winnowed down by qualified individuals and processed within the design team. It's worth the effort to take in all the ideas you can, as long as you are prepared to handle the flow effectively. Feedback should inspire and empower designers, not overwhelm them.

Avoiding design by committee should be a priority when embarking on any project. Handling the delicate balance between shutting down design drift while remaining open to all input takes skill. Key decision-makers need to be aware of the activity of the team. It is common for passionate experts to start a discussion about a new feature or a change they think would be beneficial, but it needs to be managed effectively. You don't want to kill the passion and stop great ideas from emerging, but design drift and deviations must be kept in check.

You can avoid a lot of conflict regarding feedback by creating a system and sticking to it. Establishing deadlines is effective. Requiring a well-prepared presentation of a new idea is too. Consider anything that will increase the quality of the feedback you receive.

Create standards for your design and development. If the process is consistent and well documented, people can't complain that they are being ignored or pushed aside.

*

Dealing with people is hard. Managing them is even harder. Dealing with them during the design process can be harder still. You will have people with a lot to say and those that don't like to speak at all. But the volume of the words coming out of a person's mouth shouldn't indicate the value of what they have to offer—effectively managing any process that can mutate into micromanaging or design by committee takes self-awareness, people skills, and excellent communication.

CHAPTER EIGHT

Management By Negativity

"People leave managers, not companies."
—Marcus Buckingham

A NEGATIVE MANAGER TENDS TO FOCUS on problems and not solutions. They almost always offer the stick and not the carrot. The environment in the workplace becomes severely de-energized. A manager with a negative approach has great difficulty making improvements, and any furtherance is likely the result of fear. Fear-based management is ineffective long-term.

People respond emphatically to positive managers and environments. A constructive and beneficial environment reduces stress and raises productivity. People who feel positive feel empowered and will act more readily, whereas those who think negatively will struggle with doubt, insecurity, and hesitation.

For example, you don't need an MBA from Harvard, Wharton, or Oxford to make any company in the world more profitable. Just fire a significant percentage of the workforce. This might make more profits in the short term and help the P&L look better, but the long-term impact may cost far more than the short-term benefits. Chainsaw Al Dunlap did this, and he destroyed company after company by laying off massive amounts of people. Another example of negative management is Jack Welch. During his term as chairman and CEO of General Electric, he enacted a policy where every employee was ranked yearly, and the bottom 10 percent were terminated. Talk about motivation by fear.

A business professor, Richard Boyatzis, whom I admire greatly, wrote a post in *Harvard Business Review* in May 2014. He said the most frequent question he gets from the 250,000 people enrolled in his Massive Open Online Courses (MOOC) on leadership is "How do I deal with a negative boss?"

These bosses come across as self-centered, focused on numbers, and their employees feel like they're resources, not human beings. I wonder why these people are still in management. Often, it's because their bad behavior is excused for various reasons. Maybe they perform well, brought in the most prominent client the company has ever had, or maybe their families own a large share of stock.

Sometimes we excuse these people based on organizational norms. Some policies make it difficult to fire people despite their incompetence, behavior, or other issues. You'd think with the numerous MBA programs in management education, we would have changed this dynamic by now. But sadly, empirical evidence suggests otherwise.

In one recent case, a senior leader at the C-level scheduled calls with each of his team members during the Christmas holiday. In one case, he didn't show up or reschedule. In another, he was so hungover he could barely talk; that specific call was scheduled for an hour but only lasted twenty minutes. Nevertheless, he insisted on scheduling these calls, infringing on people's personal time during an important holiday, and made it all a waste.

This same manager called his team into a meeting on a Friday afternoon and ripped everybody about how bad things were. He gave everybody huge assignments that he expected them to complete by Monday morning. Everyone worked all weekend. On Monday morning, this manager showed up at the Monday morning meeting he had scheduled and told them he didn't want to see the work. "Have a good week. See you later." And he was gone.

It was unbelievable. People busted their butts and sacrificed to get the work done, and he made all that time and effort a colossal waste. Ultimately, this negative manager self-imploded, and the organization got rid of him but only after he did a lot of damage and ruined many lives.

This same manager required us to file weekly reports, and he would often tell us how bad they were. But he never told us *why* they were bad. How can we improve without feedback? Never hearing a compliment or thank you added to the frustration.

One explanation why some managers are negative is that they are very analytical. They focus on metrics, numbers, and analyzing problems. Boyatzis talks about two different networks in your brain. One is useful for focusing, solving problems, and making decisions. When that network is activated, it suppresses what's called the default mode network (DMN). A functioning DMN is key to being open to new ideas, people, and morale issues. A suppressed DMN can cause people to become stuck. The person has trouble seeing those around them as people instead of parts of a problem they are trying to solve. Long periods of stress will inhibit their ability to renew themselves and be courteous and pleasant.

When your mind is in problem-solving mode, you're not present. Sometimes you have to step back from being hyperfocused and center on the people you're with. This requires acknowledging the problem and accepting help. We need to educate the negative managers on the impact that their negativity has on the morale and productivity of the office and coach them to change their behaviors.

One example of a negative leader I observed is Lane Kiffin, who at the time was the head coach of the varsity football team at USC. While Kiffin was at USC, I had season tickets to the football games. They were very close to the field, on about the forty-five-yard line, less than twenty rows up from the field, and

I could watch Kiffin coaching the team during games. I noticed that during games he rarely praised the players when they did something good. When they did something bad, he would aggressively launch into them. He's not the first coach to yell at a player, but he seemed to have no balance. It was management by criticism—negative management.

What really bothered me was his coaching. The people he was yelling at and berating in a stadium full of fans were kids. It's easy to forget that the 300-pound super athletes that can bench press 400 pounds are only eighteen to twenty years old. They are in a formative time of their life, and it bothered me to see him constantly criticizing them. I wasn't surprised to see Kiffin bounce from job to job. Even if I could, I would never play for him.

There are also those managers that manage using fear, and they rarely know it. Sometimes a person is not trying to make other people afraid; *they* are afraid. That fear is projected outward and into their management. They fear numerous things for many reasons, but they are often insecure. As crazy as it sounds to most of us, some managers don't want employees to achieve and soar because they might outshine them, even if the entire organization benefits. Fearful managers will clip an employee's wings that show signs of getting ahead.

It's hard not to let your personal self—your biases, beliefs, and challenges—bleed into your work life. Our management styles will be affected by our past traumas, relationships, and upbringing, as well as how we have been managed and led in the past. A fear-based manager often isn't aware of the extent to which their personal fears have saturated their management style.

They can't bring themselves to build up others. Everyone is a subordinate, and their greatest fear is a subordinate advancing past them. Since they are desperate to play the game, and their sense of self-worth is tied to it, they often advance quickly in organizations where they can make even more people miserable to feed their own insecure ego. They love rules, follow them fanatically, and punish others for a minor breach of the rules. They relish the opportunity not only to point out the flaws in others but to shine the light on their own strengths and victories.

So how do we fix this management by fear or negativity? We start by realizing that managing goes beyond HR policies. Good management requires real work with our team. We have to engage.

We must recognize that what happens at the office affects our team members' personal lives and vice versa. Make your employees feel safe.

Safety is a primal concern. No matter who we are, despite all differences, people want to feel safe. At work, job security is an important consideration of the degree of safety. A negative manager will have their people on edge, constantly worried about job security. This fear hinders open discussion and debate, stifles the environment and the entertaining of new ideas, and kills the energy that drives productivity and innovation. Being alert and on guard is exhausting and distracting, and the employee's health and well-being suffer, as well as the company's bottom line.

Making your people feel safe can be done in numerous ways. Encourage input, feedback, and new ideas. Don't criticize, penalize, or shoot down any idea—just listen. When people feel heard and respected, they feel more secure. You might be surprised at the motivation and the resulting innovation and productivity that results from this exercise alone. It could be a weekly brainstorm where everyone chimes in or a quick one-on-one. Try various approaches considering the company's size, your team, and the type of work being done.

Encourage disagreement.

You can maintain authority and gain respect even while you are encouraging people to disagree with you. People are usually hesitant to voice disagreement with the boss and won't do it if the price for doing so is high. But in our increasingly diverse world, it makes sense both ethically and fiscally to hear a comprehensive range of views. There have been major corporate gaffs recently that could have been avoided had a few more eyes looked things over before a decision was made and the execution carried out.

When there is an environment of trust and people feel safe, they are far more likely to have and sustain a conversation when disagreement occurs. When moderated effectively, these conversations can be very productive. But you need to be the model of how this collaborative effort works. Halting rampant emotions is OK; shutting down a disagreement simply because it is a disagreement is not. Many people have never learned to hear an alternate viewpoint and not take it personally. They might need to learn that from a manager.

The more trust you build, the more everyone will share their ideas. The more this occurs, the more trust is built. It's cyclical.

Don't punish people for honest mistakes.

Let your team learn from failure. An effective manager uses a misstep as a chance to teach, coach, and educate. When people are afraid to make a mistake, they become overly cautious. As a result, their creativity is stifled, and they will tend not to innovate for fear of deviating from the tried-and-true path.

Great achievers know they will make mistakes.

Employees need certain resources—don't demand performance from your team without providing them with what they need to perform. You have to know what they need. You should watch, listen, and sometimes ask. An employee afraid to ask for a new chair, for example, may spend more time avoiding sitting than working. A new chair would make them feel better, which would lead to higher productivity.

It's a collaboration. The employee is responsible for doing their job, but you are responsible for making sure they can do it. The long-term, most positive result of this is that the employees will trust you are there for them and can count on you when they need it.

Be the change you want to see.

Most important, it would be best to model the behavior you want to see in your employees. Research has shown that positive people are about 30 percent more productive and 25 percent less stressed. Thirty percent more productive! That's well worth the effort.

Examine your past communications with your team. How much had a negative focus? Did you only discuss problems? As the boss, it is on you to make this change. Review your team communications before releasing them to make sure they are positive when possible. You can address shortcomings and mistakes, but don't forget the compliments and gratitude that motivate people to keep trying to improve. As a matter of course, a fearful employee that gets overwhelmingly negative communications is far more likely to feel discouraged and demotivated.

When you do discuss problems, solicit ideas for a solution. Engage your team's creativity and show that you respect their input. Let them know that it is a team effort, and everyone has each other's back.

Recognition is an often-underutilized tool that is simple and easy to employ but can mean the world to your employees. It has been reported that only 20 percent of employees received positive recognition in a given month. However, a simple thank you can have a tremendous effect. After hearing thank you, over 90 percent of employees feel appreciated, and almost 90 percent feel happier and proud of their work.

Deborah Sweeney, CEO of MyCorporation, points out that the best managers utilize the strengths of every team member. They use emotional intelligence, not raw IQ. It is proven that many of the best leaders have high emotional intelligence, as do the top performers. It's within your power to make these changes and create a positive culture in your office. You can do that by stepping back from your analytically consumed mind on regular occasions.

*

Becoming a positive manager and building a positive environment for you and your team may feel awkward at first, but it's not difficult and well worth the effort.

CHAPTER NINE

Meetings

"Meetings move at the speed of the slowest mind in the room."

—Dale Dauten

"The five most dangerous words in business are 'Everyone else is doing it.'"

—Warren Buffett

MEETINGS ARE A KEY SOURCE OF significant stifling. While some meetings are necessary, they are often misused, mismanaged, and scheduled without ample consideration.

A recent article in *Inc.* magazine looked at a major study of meetings. Doodle interviewed more than 6,500 employees in the US, UK, and Germany. The study concluded that the cost of poorly organized meetings in 2019 was as high as $399 billion in the US and $58 billion in the UK. That's almost half a trillion dollars for just these two countries.[13]We all know what a tremendous waste

[13] Peter Economy, "A New Study of 19 Million Meetings Reveals That Meetings Waste More Time Than Ever (but There Is a Solution)," *Inc.*,

of time a meeting can be; however, few realize just how bad the problem is. One of the most detrimental consequences of poorly organized meetings is that employees have less time to do the job they are responsible for. Meetings lead to confusion, stress, and a loss of focus on projects. Irrelevant attendees often slow progress and make the meetings more inefficient.

I'll never forget one of the first meetings I had with the division president at Abbott Laboratories; I was a new marketing manager at the time. He held a monthly meeting where the other marketing managers and I had maybe five minutes each to talk about the state of our business. I was having quality problems with my products, so I told him about these problems. He hadn't heard anything about them. After the meeting, the other marketing managers confronted me. They told me—as a new marketing manager and new to the division—that I didn't understand these meetings weren't bad news meetings; these were good news meetings. The division president only wants to hear the good news!

I was astonished. I said, "I'm sorry, but if I've only got five minutes a month with this guy who's running a $2 billion business, he needs to hear what he needs to hear, whether it's good news or bad. If we have quality problems, and I can't sell my product, I need his help."

That's just an example of how a meeting can be rendered unproductive and a waste of time. Why have a meeting if the purpose is to only share the good news? I discovered that he never said that he only wanted to hear good news. That was an assumption everyone made because they feared giving the big boss bad news. Incidentally, during that meeting, the boss asked the head of manufacturing what was going on. Without his intervention, that problem would have never gotten fixed as

January 11, 2019, https://www.inc.com/peter-economy/a-new-study-of-19000000-meetings-reveals-that-meetings-waste-more-time-than-ever-but-there-is-a-solution.html.

rapidly as it did. The plant manager supported my business, but I was a lowly product manager, and he wasn't compelled to help me.

An article published in *The Economist* and posted on their website states that meetings are a necessary evil, but sometimes they seem less necessary and more evil.[14] There's a quote by the CEO of Basecamp in the article. "Meetings are like salt, sprinkled carefully to enhance a dish." Too much salt will destroy a dish, and too many meetings destroy productivity, morale, and motivation.

Excessive meetings are a drain on employees and waste company time. A Clarizen/Harris Poll survey reveals that the average American worker spends 4.5 hours in general status meetings each week and spends even longer preparing for those meetings (4.6 hours). In addition, almost half of the survey respondents stated they would rather perform some unpleasant activity, including visits to the dentist or nightmarishly long commutes, than attend status meetings.

The same article stated that CEOs spend the equivalent of two days each week in meetings, according to a study by Bain & Company, a global consulting firm. At one organization, Bain found that attendees spend 7,000 hours a year in weekly senior leadership meetings and subordinates spend 300,000 hours in related meetings and prep time.[15] I would love to provide an example, but there are just too many. Anybody that's been in business for any length of time knows the score.

Sometimes you are listening to someone that just wants to hear themselves speak. Sometimes there are meetings for the sake of having a meeting. There isn't an agenda or a defined outcome, but a meeting is scheduled whether it's needed or not.

---

[14] Terri Williams, "How to Stop Wasting Your Time—And Everyone Else's—in Meetings," *The Economist*, accessed September 16, 2021, https://execed.economist.com/blog/industry-trends/how-stop-wasting-your-time-and-everyone-elses-meetings.

[15] James Allen, "The 300,000-hour Meeting," Bain & Company, May 8, 2014, https://www.bain.com/insights/the-300000-hour-meeting-fm-blog/.

People can spend a lot of time preparing presentations for meetings. They might need to give a debrief that will last ten or twenty minutes, but they spend three or four hours preparing for it. Just tell us what we need to know. Why do we need an entire PowerPoint presentation?

Setting objectives, having a clear agenda having the right people in the room, and using technology appropriately but not excessively is the way to go. For example, when I was at Mölnlycke in 2006, my inbox was flooded with emails. People would email a large group of people, and everyone would hit reply all and weigh in with their thoughts. I was constantly emailing the people on these enormous threads and telling them to stop replying to all. I literally said, "Stop the (email, reply all, electronic debate) madness, and let's get on a call and resolve this issue."

Let's talk it out and move on. No one has time to sift through a massive number of messages spawned by the reply-all threads. It was just the culture at the time; that's how people communicated. It was not an efficient use of technology. I think we've lost the art of how useful a simple phone call can be. Let's have a conversation, make a decision, and move on.

Meetings are to a great degree now, passé. Years ago, people had to get together personally to exchange information. Today we have cell phones, texting, emails, video chat, apps, software packages, and communication and feedback portals. We can make most decisions and share information quickly without a long, drawn-out, face-to-face meeting.

To make a meeting useful, bring together only the essential people with a specific outcome in mind. A meeting can provide a forum for on-topic discussion and decision-making. Here are some tips I picked up along the way to ensure that a meeting isn't a colossal waste of time.

Necessary? Be sure the meeting has a clear goal, a purpose that can be accomplished only by hosting an event that requires people to spend company time preparing for and physically or virtually attending.

Options? Can you better accomplish your goal through some other means of communication? We are not limited to written letters and the Pony Express anymore. Most of us now hold a communication device in our pockets that is more powerful than the technology that landed men on the moon. Unfortunately, most people that carry a smartphone don't utilize it fully. Keep yourself and your people up to date on the abilities of their phones. Utilize this enormous power.

Don't forget that you can choose a hybrid of options to craft a meeting that includes people working remotely and outside of the company. Even if all parties are on-site, a short meeting can occur via video chat far quicker than assembling everyone in one place.

Attendees? Are the people you involving essential? Are they critical decision-makers? Will they aid in accomplishing the goal? Do they only need to be apprised of the content of the meeting? Can they be interviewed before the meeting or briefed after the fact? Don't involve nonessential people.

Safety? Keeping a tight focus on a meeting doesn't mean beating people into submission. Everyone should feel safe expressing opinions and offering up ideas despite being required to focus on the agenda. They can be encouraged to practice discipline and proper meeting etiquette without being oppressed.

Expectations? Make sure all participating parties know what to expect. Create a well-defined agenda and share it with everyone as soon as possible. Make sure people know why they are being asked to the meeting and what they are expected to contribute—request feedback and questions about the agenda. Answering one person's question beforehand will save time and prevent the distraction of them asking their question during the meeting.

Rules? I hate to call them rules; maybe reminders? We are not schoolchildren, but sometimes people need reminders not to use an electronic device during the meeting, not eat, or what have you. So do what you can to reasonably keep distractions to a minimum and insist that everyone present is present.

Accommodating? Consider the time zones, events, and other responsibilities of the meeting attendees as much as is reasonably possible and weigh that against the urgency of the meeting. If meeting at 10:00 a.m. requires several participants to get up at 3:00 a.m., consider a different time. Give people options ahead of time so they can all state a preference. If the meeting has a large number of attendees, you might have to list a few times and make people choose. The larger the number of people, the harder it becomes to accommodate everyone. Don't get bogged down trying to please everyone.

Focus? Keep the meeting focused and on track. Keep the talkers to a time limit, ask the introverts questions to get them talking, and encourage everyone to speak up. If good ideas pop up that are off-topic, encourage a talker to write them down and share them later. This will keep them busy and prevent them from monopolizing the meeting.

Completion? Did the meeting end with the accomplishment of the stated agenda? Keep an eye on the clock and push for a conclusion. Try to prevent having to hold another meeting.

Documentation? Make sure that the meeting is well documented, so the fruits of the meeting can be shared, learned from, and acted upon.

Things will never be perfect, so tweak and change to hone your meetings into useful events. Speak with the attendees of your meetings and hear what they have to say on the subject. Determine whether the meeting added value, had the right attendees, was the appropriate length of time, and other factors.

Now that COVID has forced us online to a great extent, here are thoughts on virtual meetings. Clearly, moving online has alleviated many problems but added a new set of challenges.

The move to virtual, online applications and technologies hasn't been without challenges but what has been accomplished in a short while has been amazing. We have already learned from this development, but from my experience, we are not managing the situation well. The pivot was fabulous, but then we went too far too fast and ended up stifling many. We have discovered or rediscovered that online meetings need to be given special attention. They are different animals.

Online meetings can cause fatigue different from that caused by physical meetings. Just being on camera can stress some people out to a great degree. Relying on technology is another stressor. In effect, you are running a small control room when you are part of an online meeting—lights, camera, action! Online meetings affect us in a very different way mentally than face-to-face meetings.

We are neither providing adequate breaks between these virtual meetings (most are back-to-back, all day long), nor are we providing time for the participants to get up and take a real break, walk around and move, grab some hydration and nourishment, or go to the bathroom. And much like being tied up in a day-long face-to-face meeting, we get stressed as the work mounts and the emails and text messages pile up.

Being on camera and seeing all those faces looking at you can be upsetting to some and distracting to others. Focusing all day on the monitor can be exhausting. Our brain is cycling through countless assessments that we aren't even aware are happening. Our senses tell us who to focus on and who to listen to in a physical meeting. Absent all our other senses, while having numerous faces looking directly at us, our minds are simultaneously overloaded with visual input while deprived of important data it needs for decision-making on a subconscious level.

Myriad camera angles and views, backgrounds, desk clutter, dress, hygiene, dogs barking, cats parading across the screen, you name it—outside the office, people let their hair down. We are also looking into their personal lives via live feed. What we see isn't the work-ready individual but the casually dressed, living-their-life person that deviates from our consistent view of them at the office. When someone jostles a camera, opens a can of soda, or clears their throat, all attention goes to them.

And many of us have forgotten that you don't have to video all meetings. It is just fine to chat the old-fashioned way, by phone and conference call. In fact, I know one executive coach who will still only coach by phone as she feels she focuses much more acutely on the conversation when she is not distracted by the visual images.

*

Meetings can be necessary, but they have become one of the most significant drains on businesses and organizations. Examine your approach to meetings, make some changes, and remove one of the biggest stiflers that exist.

CHAPTER TEN

Bureaucracy

"Bureaucracy is the art of making the possible impossible."

—Javier Salcedo

I'VE WORKED FOR SEVERAL LARGE COMPANIES and consulted with over a hundred others of all sizes. Large companies come with incredible resources and opportunities—and usually a bureaucracy. Bureaucracy has its uses, but it tends to make it very difficult to make progress and when applied too heavily. Stifling bureaucracies are out-of-date, often unnecessary, and full of redundant policies that require mountains of paperwork. They spawn red tape and often operate on mindless rigid conformity. They can be breeding grounds for some of the worst problems an organization can face, yet they are essential to the functioning of an organization.

Jerry Pournelle was an American scientist, researcher, science fiction novelist, journalist, and one of the first bloggers. He wrote Pournelle's Iron Law of Bureaucracy, which states that in any bureaucracy, the people devoted to the benefit of the bureaucracy itself always get in control, and those dedicated to the goals that the bureaucracy is supposed to accomplish have less and less influence, and sometimes are eliminated entirely.

One problem that comes with an excessive bureaucracy is that it requires individuals who function best within the rules and will mindlessly adhere to the structure. There is no room or desire for creativity, innovation, or deviation of any kind. You must do everything one way and one way only. You can see how this setup can severely handicap a company that might need to be agile and innovative in a modern, fast-paced, technologically driven market.

Ironically, a bureaucracy often demands that more people get hired to manage the growing bureaucracy, making the bureaucracy larger still, requiring even more people to manage it. Out-of-control bureaucracy is stifling at its best.

But some bureaucracy is necessary, especially in large organizations, to coordinate many people and numerous resources. But that same bureaucracy can also quickly become an impediment to the progress it was supposed to facilitate. How can we fight this? How can we ensure that a functioning bureaucracy remains useful to the organization and does not become a detriment? Let's look at the positive points of a bureaucracy, how problems can arise from that system, and how we might deal with those issues.

One way a bureaucracy can make an organization function more efficiently is by the division of labor. Getting the right people to do the job they are best qualified for makes perfect sense. But if the bureaucracy goes too far, if job descriptions become narrow and people are locked into certain roles, you might have a situation so constrictive that one person can grind a company to a halt. Hundreds, even thousands, of people can be forced to waits for the signature of one person or for a simple task to be completed.

Communication can become far more effective with proper bureaucratic oversight. A company needs to oversee communications and data in a very structured way. Some information needs to remain confidential, while other information can be put on the company website. And in today's world, easy access, secure storage, and dissemination of information are vital.

A virus, an out-of-date computer, or a misnamed file can cripple a company. Even with rigorous protocols in place and good training, hackers will still create serious problems.

While a bureaucracy can make the workplace feel impersonal, a formal relationship between the organization and the employees is usually necessary. A structured work environment and norms for behavior reduce possibly offensive situations and conflicts. It is unfortunate, but with the great diversity of the modern workplace, the litigious nature of some societies, and the fact that some employees are just not well trained, rules and guidelines must be put into place to prevent situations that can be ruinous for the organization. A massive lawsuit may very well be more stifling than a set of clear and comprehensive rules.

Many start-ups and early-stage companies have changed many rules and regulations that accompany out-of-date bureaucracies. They have done away with things like strict, formal dress codes in the workplace. But they have found that *some* guidance is necessary. Initially, as dress codes were abandoned, people arrived at work dressed inappropriately and even offensively. The response was to implement a few guidelines, but even those were open to interpretation and abuse. The rules, regulations, and policies within a bureaucracy often grow because people are very different. And sometimes, they like to cause trouble or push the boundaries. Soon, these start-ups realized that they needed to develop a fairly comprehensive dress code that covered everything from personal hygiene to what words and symbols are offensive on a shirt.

While an appropriate degree of bureaucracy can provide useful guidance and reduce situations like the distraction of a half-dressed person walking around the office, it can also reduce more severe issues like nepotism, favoritism, and bias. Only by defining a set of clear rules for the soliciting, interviewing, and hiring of people can we be sure that things are done right. When employees are chosen based on their capabilities, experience, and expertise by a diverse group, there is a far smaller chance that a misstep will occur that can cause lawsuits or other interventions.

A bureaucracy that is consistent and rational can make work less stressful and more productive for employees. Logical rules and requirements are designed to stop abuse and miscommunication. As people grow more efficient operating within the bureaucracy, their competency increases, and they can be promoted from within, thus supervising and training the new hires.

An effective bureaucracy also creates needed accountability. If people were operating at will with no approval or documentation, chaos would ensue. With adequate transparency, all levels of the bureaucracy can hold every other level—both upward and downward—accountable. I have seen this in many small companies and early-stage start-ups where everyone is running so hard and so fast that fundamental systems and processes get ignored.

It is often a real pain, but one benefit of a bureaucracy is that it slows things down. We don't want to halt progress, which can sometimes be the case, but a speed bump is usually a good idea as it can stop a poor decision from being made. It's smart to consider options and research and include as many viewpoints as practical in decisions. There's usually a well-justified reason that a more experienced higher-up needs to sign off on major decisions.

There are disadvantages to bureaucracy. Red tape is one of the big ones. Red tape is an idiom that people use when rules and regulations become excessive and when requirements are overly rigid, redundant, or just ridiculous and hinder productivity.

Sometimes activities such as filling out a form or obtaining a signature are called red tape, but just because someone doesn't feel like filling out a form doesn't mean it is ridiculous and unnecessary. But if a person must fill out the same information numerous times, technology should be employed. There's no reason to enter the same data more than once these days. And the more someone must write the same information, the greater the chance of inconsistencies and inaccuracies occurring.

Another disadvantage of the bureaucracy is the tendency for the individual bureaucrats to stay in their own lane. Transparency and awareness are greatly restricted when individuals are allowed to operate unmonitored in a bubble. Unfortunately, some people abuse this situation.

An hourly clerk can hold up a massive project by dragging their feet. Some people enjoy that sense of power and exercise it whenever they can for their self-satisfaction. A bureaucracy can become toxic when people who desire excessive control are operating in the structure. Managers who don't trust the people below them to operate independently will insist on a highly defined set of rules, processes, and procedures that must be signed off on by the higher-ups. This is where a lot of the stifling occurs.

I once worked for a large, global medical device company. We needed to choose a customer relationship management (CRM) solution for our location. What should have been a simple and straightforward decision became a long, frustrating ordeal. Some people wanted to have control over the decision from a centralized standpoint. This was just a CRM in a local market. We had qualified people that were more than capable of making this decision, but corporate headquarters wanted to control the decision. So, we waited and waited to be told what to do. Why did they insist on having the power to make this decision when the decision did not directly affect them? Yes, I recognize that other markets may wish to use the same CRM and the benefit of standardization. We wasted a lot of time waiting, working in limbo while this individual, and ultimately a team, insisted on getting involved with a local decision. It was very stifling and totally unnecessary.

Another serious issue that can occur in a bureaucracy is corruption, and it can occur at all levels. From the expectation of small cash payments and gifts to make sure a form doesn't get lost in the system to large-scale corruption at higher levels. Corruption in a bureaucracy at any level can be disastrous. Imagine the lowest level clerk in charge of processing certain forms deciding whose forms land on the bosses' desk—if at all. One clerk could endanger an entire institution if they singled out a certain group of people and treated them according to a personal bias. Running afoul of federal law, even due to the actions of one person, could put the entire organization in jeopardy.

When a bureaucracy is run inefficiently and delivers consistently poor results, people will try to adapt and create workarounds. They will anticipate the poor results and will pad their requests. They will ask for more money, time, and resources than they need to get what they actually need. Without clean, accurate data, an organization will malfunction.

There are so many ways that people can stifle those above and below them in a bureaucracy that it takes skill to ensure that it runs smoothly. Of course, it is often the bureaucrat's inclination to add more bureaucracy to fix a problem within a bureaucracy. This is like adding more waterpipe rather than fixing a leak. The answer isn't to add more bureaucracy but to lessen it, streamline it, remove redundancies, and encourage more visibility of the activities of each part of the system. Tom Hodgson, the chief operating officer during most of my career at Abbott Laboratories, used to say, "Be careful when you hire people as they will want to do something and that something is not always in the best interest of the business."

A major investment bank forced its investment bankers to convert client's public financial data obtained on Bloomberg to a proprietary spreadsheet format. They had to do this by hand, one at a time. Finally, one banker who knew how to program wrote software that automatically converted the Bloomberg terminal data into the proprietary worksheets. His initiative saved the company an enormous amount of time and money.

Shortly after, this same banker had more ideas, and when he approached his direct manager with these ideas, he was scolded and told to "Stop innovating," go back to his cubicle and get back to work. This person had stepped out on their own, saved the company untold amounts of time and money, but when he tried to do it again, their response was to stop innovating! This is bureaucracy at its worst and one of the biggest dangers of a rigid bureaucracy and stifling managers. That focus on the way it's supposed to be done as opposed to how we can do it better is one of the major problems with bureaucracy. This banker voted with his feet and left the company. This same manager working high up some sixty floors in an office building tossed his car keys to the same banker and asked him to go down to the parking garage and get his sunglasses because it was too sunny in his office! Very nice touch, Mr. manager!

No one in a rigid bureaucracy such as the one just mentioned is coaching the managers, watching their behavior, or keeping an eye on the big picture. For the most part, people are focused on cranking the bureaucratic machine forward because doing anything else would bring unwanted attention. If they can keep the wheels moving in the narrowly prescribed way, they can run their teams the way they want to. Employees end up being subservient drones because that's the way the manager wants it. Creativity, experimentation, innovation, and anything that doesn't move the hamster wheel are not welcomed.

In one company I worked for, we had to create weekly reports, and all we got back was harsh criticism from the manager. He never told us what was wrong with them or what we could do differently. Instead, he'd say, "This isn't what I'm looking for." We asked many times, "What is it you're looking for?" He never answered us. We tried many approaches. We even asked his admin to give us help figure out what he was looking for. We never got any answers.

So, what were we supposed to do? We acquiesced. We were demoralized, frustrated, and felt like children doing busy work. This was a team of considerable education, experience, and ability squandered because of this nonsense. We had no recourse.

I had another manager, specifically not listed in the appendix, who used to mark up our monthly comments with colored felt tip pens and return them to us for rework. The last time I had been exposed to that was thirty-six years earlier by my second-grade teacher, Ms. French.

To be a functioning environment, people need to feel safe speaking up, calling out problems and mistakes, and offering suggestions for improvement without the fear of retribution or ridicule. And they need to know their input will be considered and acted upon.

Let people out of their confined bubbles, encourage them to be conscious of the system they are a part of. How does it affect you, how do you affect it, and what can be done to make it better?

But what needs to be better? In a creative environment, a higher degree of mistakes needs to be tolerated, even encouraged. There's no way around it—the process of creativity and innovation demands experimentation. A manager might see wasted resources, failed efforts, and wasted time, but in the creative process, this is progress. Of course, there are situations where you can't afford the risk of abandoning a rigid structure. Hazardous work environments, the medical field, and other such situations require strict adherence to certain standards and rules.

*

Most people show up to work wanting to do a good job. They want to feel valued. So let them be creative and see what comes of it. Everyone's big complaint about millennials is they don't want to be managed, but my attitude is to get the hell out of their way and shield them from bureaucracy whenever possible. Let them use their creative juices and their paradigms. Let them use the technology they grew up with. Let them work, and then sit them down and see what they did. Tell them what's good or what you'd like to see changed.

CHAPTER ELEVEN

Performance Reviews

"Performance Management isn't dead. The old way of thinking about it is."

—Anita Bowness

ALMOST NO ONE LIKES ANNUAL PERFORMANCE reviews. They're stressful, tedious, and essentially useless. The Society for Human Resource Management reports that 95 percent of employees are unhappy with their company's review process.[16] A recent Gallup poll states that only 14 percent of employees strongly agree that performance reviews inspire them to improve.[17] In addition, these annual reviews cost an organization a lot of money; for a large

---

[16] Allen Smith, "More Employers Ditch Performance Appraisals," Society for Human Resource Management, May 18, 2018, https://www.shrm.org/resourcesandtools/legal-and-compliance/employment-law/pages/more-employers-ditch-performance-appraisals.aspx.

[17] Jennifer Robinson, "7 Quick Tips to Help Managers Salvage Annual Reviews," Gallup, October 9, 2020, https://www.gallup.com/workplace/321674/quick-tips-help-managers-salvage-annual-reviews.aspx.

company with 10,000 employees, that cost can range from $2 to $5 million a year. Nevertheless, companies get consumed and paralyzed by this process, stifling the employees in the process.

So why do we keep doing them the way we always have? Mainly because we've always done them that way. Modern corporate culture has stagnated in many respects, and the performance review is one of them. Everyone does them, no one likes them, and no one believes they're beneficial. Yet, with all the data advocating the elimination of these annual performance reviews, many companies are still doing them.

Elton Mayo, a psychologist, and organizational theorist, often considered the father of HR theory, established a model for employee engagement that was an alternative to Frederick Winslow Taylor's rigid scientific management approach. It was a positive change at the time, and it started the trend toward more human-centered performance-based management. "Using feedback on performance to course-correct once a year, or even twice a year, is akin to trying to navigate a minefield by reviewing your performance after you've crossed it. . .only on this minefield, the landmines are shifting underground as you walk through them!"[18] In other words, if you're only going to give me feedback once or twice a year, why bother giving me any feedback at all?

Performance reviews started during WWI and have evolved little over the years. Recently, change has been forced to occur, but many organizations still maintain the archaic methods of the performance review. Thus, a once innovative tool has become a significant stifler to many organizations. When they first came out over a hundred years ago, they were quite revolutionary, but the world has changed a lot since then.

Some companies have begun to do away with the traditional performance review, and it is no surprise that these companies

---

[18] Thomas Koulopoulos, "Performance Reviews Are Dead. Here's What You Should Do Instead," *Inc.,* May 11, 2021, https://www.inc.com/gabrielle-bienasz/sprinly-ray-lui-family-sacrifice-discrimination.html.

are in the tech sector, where they must remain agile and quick moving. In the past, the employment track for an individual was one where a person could start at the bottom and move upward, learning along the way. However, recently, it is more common that a new employee must start as a fully functioning team member with a specialized job with an ever-evolving skillset. Therefore, the notion of a yearly review being of any benefit is ludicrous if that is the only portion of a review process.

More than ever, companies are dependent on very bright individuals—agile learners that can keep up with and even anticipate industry trends. Unfortunately, these new employees often lack real-world work experience and need adequate and full-time coaching and mentorships. Without it, employees feel underappreciated, neglected, and are ripe for poaching with the promise of more money and perks.

Technology moves at such a rapid and unpredictable rate that creative and innovative thinking is a significant advantage in the marketplace. Still, high-energy creativity requires a firm yet gentle hand to keep it on track while not stifling it. The delicate balance between individual creativity, team collaboration, and organizational goals requires an experienced but agile manager to guide and nurture the organization's efforts consistently. This is supported by another Gallup poll that shows that the results of weekly versus annual feedback. Team members are 5.2 times more likely to "strongly agree" that they received meaningful feedback, 3.2 times more likely to "strongly agree" that they're motivated to do outstanding work, and 2.7 times more likely to be engaged at work.[19]

So, what is required of these new-school managers? Managers must be in touch with their team consistently. Management by walking around is required. You don't want to micromanage, but being available, being present, and having informal chats regularly

[19] Robert Sutton and Ben Wigert, "More Harm Than Good: The Truth About Performance Reviews," Gallup, May 6, 2019, https://www.gallup.com/workplace/249332/harm-good-truth-performance-reviews.aspx.

will give you many opportunities to monitor performance and suggest minor adjustments along the way. It is also great for employees as they will know that you are available and care about them. It allows them to communicate with you and head off potential performance issues. Millennials are especially keen on career development and will welcome this approach.

There are also many software packages and apps that allow for real-time performance tracking. These apps allow everyone to collect and track input from multiple sources such as management, subordinates, customers, and vendors. Input mechanisms can be set up as fill-in-the-blanks, multiple-choice, and quizzes, to name a few. Data can be processed and presented in various ways for an up-to-date image of the employee's performance. Negative trends can be seen and addressed and problems headed off early and more frequently.

Google uses a team-based approach. One strength of this approach is that no one can easily manipulate it. In addition, multiple team members create a system of checks and balances that will potentially prevent biased and myopic decisions from being made. Many companies are moving to a team-based review process because it's far more comfortable, transparent, and safer for the employee when an individual's career isn't in the hands of only one or perhaps two people immediately above them in the pecking order.

We still need employee performance tracking and review, but we need it in a form that adequately serves the present-day workers and workplace. The latest trend is the real-time 360-review process, where feedback is collected on an employee from subordinates, colleagues, managers, and the employee. Sources of feedback can also include customers, suppliers, or anyone the employee interacts with.

This is currently the best process, I believe. Rather than the yearly review, this is a constant, ongoing process of review and improvement. This new approach provides feedback from numerous sources, a full circle of feedback (360 degrees). Everyone an employee interacts with is a potential source, and the feedback is collected on an ongoing basis. It's not as overwhelming as it sounds. Once it is in place, it is a seamless part of the job. Momentum and workflow aren't disrupted nearly as much as a yearly performance review.

We start with an established and standard set of criteria such as questions and a rating system. Then the employee is monitored for effectiveness, the success of interactions, communication skills, consistency, timeliness, and much more. The group that will be reviewing the employee can be broadly defined and should include a wide spectrum to be most effective. When all employees constantly evaluate each other in small increments, you get a full detailed and up-to-date picture of the employee's performance.

You can also immediately investigate any anomalies that surface. For example, one employee, who might get stellar ratings from all the members of his universe, always gets terrible ratings from one source. You look closer and establish that this source doesn't give terrible ratings to any other employee. You have uncovered what is possibly an issue between two people. It could be any number of things, but the key here is to handle it immediately. Is it the employee or the source that is at fault? You can immediately and accurately identify and address an issue rather than waiting for it to turn into a more significant and more serious problem.

Set up your own system and experiment. Then, with small doses of feedback recorded over time, you can build an accurate image of your organization. You will get lots of useful information from this approach.

Make sure you start with qualified people setting up the system and reviewing the feedback. Both you and your employees will need to be trained in the most effective way to give and receive feedback. Getting raw feedback about yourself can be upsetting. It will make most people immediately defensive, but with proper training, they should understand that the feedback is not a threat. Also, when an employee understands that negative feedback from one individual won't get them fired, it's easier to hear.

This process is meant for all levels. Managers and leaders can find this system incredibly enlightening. Management rarely gets unfiltered feedback from those around them, especially those they manage. The feedback gleaned from the 360-review process can be hard to process, and the view might be uncomfortable, but you will learn a lot and improve immensely from the experience.

The 360-process doesn't remove the need for periodic chats and meetings about performance issues. But it gives management more data to serve the organization. For example, instead of every employee getting thirty minutes a year of review, some high-performing employees may require less time than those who need more guidance.

The most important thing we can do for our employees and organizations is to create an atmosphere where people want to develop and help them do so. If we provide a range of resources such as training, coaching, and counseling, they will utilize it to grow. If we are good mentors and show that we care deeply for and actively develop our employees, they will flourish and help us develop.

Some argue that if you hire good people, you shouldn't need to train or develop them much further. This may have been true in the past when the work environment changed at a much slower rate. However, today, even the brightest and most prepared employees need ongoing development and training to keep up.

Part of creating a positive work atmosphere is being available. Many executives are proud of their open-door policies, but they may as well be sitting in a locked bank vault. Most people are intimidated by their managers and don't want to disturb them. So, managers need to walk around, engage, and get to know their people if they want to build rapport and be open and accessible. This is something I was encouraged to do early on. One of my first jobs was in hospital administration at Ochsner Hospital in New Orleans back in 1981. We had weekly executive management meetings with the CEO, David Pitts, and his staff. David assigned each member of the executive team a unit that he expected us to visit at least once a week. I came up knowing the benefits of this approach. In my last role at Mölnlycke Health Care, we had about sixty employees in our US headquarters in Atlanta. I still got out of my office at least once a day and walked around and talked to as many people as was practical. The key was to make myself approachable and available.

If you are interested in implementing a 360-performance review system, the most often repeated advice is to make sure that you don't give it a half measure. Hire a consultant if you need to because setting up a system like this can be complex, and doing it wrong can cause more harm than good. But once it is in place, a well-functioning 360 system is almost seamless and a lot less painful.

The changeover from a leader/manager-centric performance review model to a full spectrum employee assessment system can be uncomfortable. But developing a workplace where culture thrives and employees are more productive makes it worth the investment of time and money.

Here's what is typically involved in setting up a 360 system.

First, you need to assess your company—size, culture, mission, and goals. And from those, various tools are implemented throughout the organizational structure and at every critical junction of the business. This data is formatted for storage and future examination. The tools might be questionnaires sent to customers after an interaction with a member of the organization, a weekly form that team members fill out regarding their peers, or another performance measure. These tools are meant to integrate into the everyday operations of the organization. Part of what makes the system effective is that it prevents the employee from being on the spot as a manager asks questions. The result of an integrated system like this is more accurate data that is sampled constantly from various inputs. The results are an order of magnitude more complete than a spreadsheet of metrics and figures. This is one reason the best person to review and discuss the data collected may not be the direct supervisor or manager of the employee but an impartial third party. The discussions will be more relaxed and honest. This should be a confidential meeting where the employee can speak their mind and not fear any repercussions.

These interviews should focus on the coworkers, managers, and the culture. You want to build an accurate image of your employee's experiences in your organization. Themes will emerge from the data, potential problems, bottlenecks, and so much more. Improvement will be so much easier, and you will find that correcting some of the easiest issues will reap the biggest results.

A professional interviewer will be adept at putting people at ease and asking questions in a fashion that will reveal information. For example, instead of going straight for the jugular and asking the employee what they dislike about the boss, they might ask questions about the areas the boss is responsible for. If the question is asked, "Do you ever feel uncomfortable in the office?" the resulting reaction will be telling. If all is well, the response will most likely be a clarifying question about the temperature, their chair, or something more benign. That's easy to address. If something more serious is happening, the response will usually be silence and a troubled expression as the individual grapples with what to say. Then well-crafted follow-up questions will help lead to possibly critical information. With all this data, you can more easily detect potential problems early on.

When you gather information on the culture of the workplace, the data should be shared, in some form, with all the employees. Employees want to be heard, even if their concerns aren't acted upon. Employees will feel respected and empowered if the results of the collected data pertaining to the workplace and culture are acted upon. They will know that the leadership is listening and cares.

And you need to take action. If all this data is collected and goes unused, it is a waste. And more, it can be frustrating and even insulting to employees to participate in this collection of data, then hears nothing come of it. It is critical to communicate what the plans are for the data, when and what will be presented, and what will be done about the findings. When employees are involved by hearing the plans and being part of the changes, they feel invested and even loyal to the business.

Designing and implementing a 360-degree review process can be awkward at first, and employees may grumble, but this process facilitates the servant leadership model very well. The employees will quickly adapt to the system and appreciate the results it produces. Managers and leaders will have the ability to solve problems, analyze operational efficiencies, and troubleshoot issues when they are just starting.

*

We're in the midst of a revolution. The pace of the marketplace and the nature of the work demands that we develop people and give them feedback immediately. The old management paradigm of annual targets and performance reviews is obsolete. The need for ongoing coaching is now not only practical but also vitally required. Younger generations want to grow, learn, and develop in their careers. They want to stay relevant, useful, and up to date on technology and trends. They will do this largely on their own and can be a great asset to whatever organization they belong to. Some companies now encourage their young employees to mentor senior executives in a reverse mentoring process.

One thing is for sure—a millennial won't wait around for a year to be told they are doing a good job.

CHAPTER TWELVE

The Servant Leader

"As we look ahead into the next century, leaders will be those who empower others."

— Bill Gates

"Keep morale up, keep people motivated."

—Margaret Thatcher

It is always the right time to do the right thing.

—Martin Luther King, Jr.

ROBERT GREENLEAF COINED THE SERVANT LEADER model in an essay published in 1970. It's a concept that many people ascribe to, but it's hard to carry out. I think some people misunderstand the original intention of this term and have flipped it to mean I'm going to give my people whatever they want. That was never the intention.

The concept of servant leadership has been around for a very long time. Greenleaf defined it as "The servant leader is servant first. . .it begins with the natural feeling that one wants to serve, to serve first. Then conscious choice brings one to aspire to lead. That person is sharply different from one who is leader first, perhaps because of the need to assuage an unusual power drive or to acquire material possessions."[20]

The servant leader is focused on the team members. They are interested in the growth and prosperity of the team, organizations, and communities they are members of. Unfortunately, too many leaders are focused on amassing wealth, power, and privilege. They believe they are at the top of the power pyramid and the people below are their servants. The servant leader may know that they hold authority and can direct those below them in the pecking order of an organization, but they are there to help those that follow; they share the power and the benefits of success, knowing it is a team effort. They want to help people develop and perform because they know it will benefit the entire organization.

If you can change your mindset to that of the servant leader—if you're not already there—you will benefit as much or more than the employees you serve. As you empower your employees with respect and trust, they empower you and the organization with higher degrees of loyalty, conscientiousness, and motivation.

A study by Sen Sendjaya and James C. Sarros in 2002 concluded that some of the top-ranked companies in the world practice the servant leader model.[21] More recently, servant leadership has been very popular in the technological sector, and it makes sense. As we discussed in other parts of this book, employees today need to be empowered to stay current and work more efficiently. This leads to how teams and projects are managed.

Agile management methodologies are widely used in technology organizations, so projects can iterate quickly and adapt

---

[20] Robert K. Greenleaf, "The Servant as Leader," Greenleaf.org, accessed September 16, 2021.

[21] Sen Sendjaya and James C. Sarros, "Servant Leadership: Its Origin, Development, and Application in Organizations," *Journal of Leadership & Organizational Studies* 9, no: 2 (September 2002): 57-64.

when needed. Agile is a quick-moving process where frequent client interaction and collaborative decision-making allow for quick changes and adaptability. Traditional methods of project management cannot accommodate these differences effectively. To work, agile requires team members that are independent, knowledgeable, and decisive. Regardless of the degree of independence an employee has attained, the role of leader is still vital.

To serve in the role of a servant leader, as opposed to supreme commander, requires humility. But humility doesn't mean that a leader is powerless or disrespected. The true servant leader has great power and respect. Followers of the effective servant leader can be fiercely loyal and use their potential, creativity, and purpose toward the mutual goal of organizational success. It's a win-win, not leader wins, and followers get the crumbs.

Traditional management is often described as transactional, meaning that employees exchange their time and effort for pay. In addition, this management style is positional, meaning they are the boss based solely on their position in the pecking order. On the other hand, the servant leader transcends this traditional transactional arrangement and instead develops and aligns the employees' goals and aspirations with those of the company.

Advocates of the servant leader model note that empowered employees perform at levels much higher than those in traditional leadership structures. This kind of change starts from the top down. The leadership must want this and have an unselfish mindset. The entire organization must be invested in this change of culture. People may walk as the changes occur, but you will also attract higher-quality talent as word of the changes of the organization gets out. Finally, there are the individuals that need to practice these new behaviors constantly. Servant leaders cannot be hypocritical, manage by negativity, or allow any incivility or bullying in the workplace. The servant leader's goal is to remove stifles from their organization, so a misunderstanding of the servant leader model can end up being more of a stifle than not.

I once worked with someone who misunderstood the servant leadership model. He empowered his team by giving them everything they wanted but also overrode the managers and subrogated the authority he'd given them. He promoted trust, integrity, and honesty as a foundation to his results model pyramid. But he routinely lied to my face and went back on his word. He was a terrible steward of the company's resources. He served his team by giving them whatever they wanted in terms of pricing for their customers. But there was no pricing strategy, and things fell apart.

He took care of his team at the expense of the organization. It got so bad that if a sales representative asked their manager for dispensation, and the manager said no, the sales rep would go straight to the president and get whatever they wanted. Pricing was a complete disaster when I took over that business. Servant leader doesn't mean giving your people everything they want, whenever they want it, and however they want it.

The impact of adopting the servant leader model can be immensely positive, so let's explore the basic guidelines for those who wish to become servant leaders.

Servant leadership is already a global and historical concept. It has roots in Eastern and Western culture and goes back as far as the fifth century BC. Lao Tzu wrote, "The highest type of ruler is one of whose existence the people are barely aware."

Southwest Airlines is often called a modern example of servant leadership. The founder, Herb Kelleher, is the personification of a servant leader. Kelleher began by placing the good of his employees over his own interests, including their personal and professional development. By all accounts, Kelleher viewed all employees of Southwest as equal in the organization. As proof of this dedication to servant leadership, let's look at Colleen Barrett.

Colleen Barrett was a legal secretary when she started working with Kelleher at the start of Southwest Airlines. She had no degree or formal management training but became president of Southwest Airlines in 2001. To date, Barrett is the only woman who has ever held that position for a major airline. Unquestionably, she earned her place, but Herb Kelleher acted as a true servant leader and helped her get there. Barrett stepped down in 2008 but has served as president emerita of the airline.

Kelleher always puts employees first. Barrett describes Southwest Airline's structure as employees being at the top of the power pyramid. Empowered employees are motivated to treat the customer far better. Satisfied customers are repeat customers and the best marketing a company can get—word-of-mouth promotion. The stakeholders are happy because they are profiting from the process. Barrett estimated she spends 80 to 90 percent of her time ensuring that employees are supported in their jobs and that customers are happy.

Herb Kelleher and Colleen Barrett led a major organization successfully, turning a profit for over three decades when most in the industry do not, with a highly engaged and loyal workforce. Southwest Airlines is the model of servant leadership.

The practice of transforming an organization to the servant leader model starts with the core principle we've already looked at: servant leaders desire to serve their staff. But where do you go from here? You will need to implement many organization-wide changes and simultaneously enact them, but let's start with hiring new employees.

Catch them early. Changing the existing culture is hard enough; don't let the new hires take on any old ways. Start with your job postings, screening, and interviewing process. After a new employee is onboarded, they should be asked about their thoughts on the people they've met, observations they've made, and impressions they've formed of the organization. Get them used to giving their opinions from the start. Knowing their opinion is valued is the first step into making an engaged and productive employee that will ask for what they want, point out problems, and feel invested in an organization.

Keep track of the employee's desire for advancement and their personal development needs. Anything from their health goals, long-term personal visions, and day-to-day issues should be recorded and addressed. Show your people there is a growth environment, and the organization will support their journey. Sincere and consistent support generates deep loyalty to an organization. One rule of thumb is that if a manager is not spending at least 25 percent of their time developing their people, they're failing as a leader. Personally, I think in some instances, it should be more than that.

When a servant leader develops their people, they know their strengths, weaknesses, goals, and desires. We all know the story of the two chefs working in the same restaurant. Both chefs needed an orange for their dish, but there was only one orange to be had. They fought over the orange, and an hour later, they decided to cut the fruit in half. They each finished their dishes with less than what they needed, and the results were that neither made the best dish they could have. The thing is, one of their recipes called for the meat of the orange and the other the entire peel. Had they communicated better, they both would have succeeded.

One goal of a servant leader is to empower their people, which also implies giving up some power. Employees, especially today, need to be prepared and confident enough to take the initiative. If you equate leadership with control, this might be hard to do, but you will find you will actually have more control if you let go. Once your people utilize their strengths and shore up their weaknesses, are fully engaged and capable, you can direct your organization quickly and precisely to meet your goals and fulfill the organization's vision.

Learning to let go and lead is probably the hardest thing for the traditional leader, but it is critical. If a leader can't do this, they can't be a servant leader, and the entire model ceases to function.

As a servant leader, how do you know who needs help and what they need? You listen, you ask questions, and you listen some more. People in a traditional work environment need time and training to get used to giving and receiving feedback. They will need to get used to the fact that you want them to give their opinions, raise their concerns, and not just "shut up and work." Most important, people need to learn to function in this new environment; you need to develop a strategy to reign back the excessive talkers and inciters and get the introverts to participate.

Soliciting an opinion from an employee isn't asking them to tell you what to do; it is getting input. Sometimes, adults don't understand this. For example, some people think that if you ask them what color the walls should be, and they say black, you will paint the walls black. So, manage expectations. Encourage more questions, ask more questions, clarify the answers. Make sure there is an understanding of what the process will be moving forward.

As a servant leader builds people's trust, they will learn more about each employee, their hopes and dreams, struggles, and achievements. Take it all in. They will feel respected; you will be better informed and better able to serve them. Ask them about the work environment, their view of the industry, and what might help them perform their job more effectively. Ask about the employee facilities, their take on how meetings are run, and more. As you gain the trust of the workforce, they will speak more freely and openly. Once they know that their words won't be used against them and get the message that you really want to hear their opinions, you will feel like you have sensors in every nook and cranny of the business. You'll be able to make minor adjustments that head off potentially major problems. Best of all, you will have a workforce that is respected, invested, and motivated.

Listening is an art and can be a big adjustment for someone who talks most of the time. The traditional model expects people to keep their mouths shut and listen. Under the servant leader model, it is the opposite. Listening takes patience, and hearing takes practice. First, you'll learn to pick up on what's not being said and what questions to ask to bring that information to light. Then, you'll recap. Finally, explaining your understanding of what was said will give both you and the team member a chance to clarify.

Proper listening is mostly good old-fashioned manners. For example, being fully engaged and not looking at your phone or watch repeatedly during a conversation. Instead, make eye contact, admit when your attention drifts and apologize, but keep the conversation going.

So, you are talking, listening, and your workforce is giving you reams of information—the employee bathroom is always dirty, our tools are out of date, I have an idea of how we can save money on shipping, my manager's breath stinks, my dog turned twelve today. Now what?

Servant leaders listen then respond. Do not react—respond. "Thank you for this information." "Someone will follow up with you soon." "I will speak with so-and-so." "Tell your dog happy birthday from me." The proper response is powerful, but it doesn't have to solve problems on the spot. You want people to know that they are being heard, not expect to be obeyed. You are a servant leader, not a servant.

Whatever the interaction, be calm and listen; take it all in. Resist the negative urge to explain, confront, or defend. Likewise, resist the well-meaning desire to make promises. Don't take any action or commit until you have more input, hear all sides, and consider all your options and the consequences. Stay positive and encouraging. Take notes and act later. Foster an environment where productive and calm conversations take place. You will find that employees are often more able to help than they need help.

Trust is the core of the servant leadership model. The leader must trust the employees, and the employees must trust the leader.

*

Successfully implementing and practicing servant leadership can be a hard road to start down, but the benefits are immense and well worth the effort. Trusted employees, who've earned that trust, will be inspired and flourish. The leader that can do this will be the captain of a boat where all crew members are happily rowing in the same direction with all they've got.

As Stephen Covey says, "Trust is one of the means to achieve servant leadership, and it is also an end that is achieved by servant leadership."[22]

[22] Mark Tarallo, "The Art of Servant Leadership," Society for Human Resource Management, May 17, 2018, https://www.shrm.org/resourcesandtools/hr-topics/organizational-and-employee-development/pages/the-art-of-servant-leadership.aspx.

CHAPTER THIRTEEN

Workplace Politics

"I gotta get outta here. I think I'm gonna lose it."

—Peter Gibbons

"When elephants fight, it is the grass that gets trampled."

—African Proverb

"It's that whale that surfaces which gets harpooned."

—J. Duncan McIntyre

WORKPLACE POLITICS CONJURE UP NEGATIVE SCENARIOS; people are gossiping, and some are engaging in manipulative behavior to achieve their own selfish goals. Office politics can be a big stifler to an organization. Let's talk about how you deal with workplace politics as a boss or an employee.

You can't ignore office politics. They can be elusive, slippery, and complex to deal with, but deal with it you must. Wherever you are on the organization chart, office politics will find you. Keeping your head down and doing your job will most likely keep you out of trouble at lower levels, but it can also prevent you from making progress in your career. At the upper levels of management, you don't have such luxury.

No matter who you are, undoubtedly, something about you will draw the eye of the office gossip. Race, gender, religion, sexual orientation, gender identity, income, education, height, weight, attractiveness—the list is endless. But separate from the serious issues of discrimination and bias, I am talking about these differences in the context of office politics. Why? Because if you feel that accusations are being aimed at you, such as doing inappropriate things to the top, filling a quota, or somehow didn't earn your position, you need to deal with it effectively. Don't be rash; study the situation.

If people are talking about you behind your back, they might be shy or afraid. People often try to get answers from a secondary source to avoid the discomfort of the straightforward approach. You may need to approach them to quell the talk with answers.

We are in delicate territory so let me be very clear. I am not suggesting that you tolerate even the smallest amount of discrimination, incivility, or poor treatment. My point is that we are all human, and sometimes we misunderstand, speak out of ignorance, or make mistakes. My goal here is to help you effectively deal with politics in the workplace and come out on top by avoiding nasty situations by communicating. I am by no means telling you to tolerate anything that isn't ethical, moral, legal, and comfortable for you.

That being said, office politics can sometimes be taken to a level that can only be described as evil. Sometimes the people that partake in such behavior can rise to the top. It is frustrating to watch a political animal leapfrog past you based on their charm while you work hard. But don't be distracted. The problem isn't the charming ladder climber but the organization that allows for their advancement. And you are not powerless. Some of the responsibility falls on you to navigate the situation.

No one should be promoted for their good looks alone or held back for an irrelevant or illegal reason. Still, as much as you might find the charmer that skates past you on the career track distasteful, you might want to study what they are doing before condemning them too quickly. Why? Because you might have misread the situation.

Bob Burg, the author of *Endless Referrals,* is famous for a quote that explains why the ladder climber may be more than just superficial charm. "All things being equal, people do business with and refer business to people they know, like, and trust." The charming person understands this or naturally operates in this way, which might be why you are left behind.

Organizations are groups of people who must function well together, which requires knowing, liking, and trusting each other. That takes effort. Suppose a person is nurturing relationships, seeking mentors, showing interest in the organization, getting involved, and performing their duties successfully. In that case, they are doing things right and deserve no criticism. But if this person is not doing their work and somehow manipulating their way to the top, that's a totally different situation.

In the first situation, advancement was earned. When a person gets to know you well, likes you, and trusts you, you will be uppermost in their mind when an opportunity presents itself. This makes logical sense in any situation you apply it to, from hiring a babysitter to choosing an accountant. Honest self-reflection is a tool we talked about earlier, and this is one situation where it can serve you well.

Being effective at getting people to know, like, and trust you isn't office politics. My good friend and past coworker, Peter Karas, Jr., loved to say, "When times are good, people do business with people they like. When times are bad, people do business with people they like."

Unfortunately, discrimination, bias, and favoritism exist in the world, be it conscious or not. You need to be savvy to get past some of these hurdles that shouldn't even exist. Realize that just because you share some of the same traits as another person in the office doesn't automatically make them your ally. In fact, they might view you as their competition. Conversely, people very different from you can surprise you with their support and loyalty. Keep your eyes open.

Choose your allies well. Ask yourself who can make or break you career-wise? Who can refer you for a new opportunity or invite you to the events that get you noticed? And who does your boss depend on? Befriending an executive assistant or another person that your boss relies on can be a tremendous advantage.

This might feel a bit smarmy if you believe that you should be judged solely on your merits and qualifications, but there is merit to building relationships and trust. At higher levels of management, you are no longer performing a job that can be done in relative isolation. People need to know, like, and trust you to give you greater responsibility.

Other aspects of office politics can be unspoken, unwritten, and unofficial. There are accepted norms, ways of doing things, and ways of being in workplace culture. If you are a literal thinker, a rules and numbers person, and think about how things "should" be, you need to practice looking for this undocumented culture. Look for the people who seem to command respect or attention despite their position. Study the people who are advancing quickly. If the top performers dress professionally, show up early, and never forget an important event in the boss's life, follow suit. Performing within the confines of your job description will confine you to that job. Higher-ups want to see that you are interested in advancement and taking the initiative before they will advance you. Too many people are relentlessly focused on their next job; you are much better off doing your current job as well as you can.

Again, I must distinguish between right and wrong activity. As you study your workplace, you will also determine if the criteria for advancement are unethical or illegal. If it is, that requires a different tact than dealing with office politics. I am not advocating that you tolerate any demeaning, unethical, or illegal treatment or anything you find objectionable.

But how do you handle a situation that might be challenging but one that you want to stay in? First, stay calm. Be aware that how you react to anything is a message to those around you. Do you fold into a ball of victimization? Do you get defensive? Do you acquiesce too easily? No matter what you feel, like the old ad says, never let them see you sweat. You always have a choice as to how you react. Stephen Covey has some great advice in his book, *The 7 Habits of Highly Effective People.* It's a few years old now but still full of relevant and valuable information.

Don't react; respond later when you are calm and have a more accurate read on the situation. Holding back a reaction also gives you valuable time to consider your long-term goals and plan a response tailored to what you are trying to achieve. For example, if someone has made a remark you found offensive, you can escalate the situation and file a complaint with HR; you could react on the spot with a reprimand, demand an apology, or fire back a similar remark, or you could walk away and think. If the remark was a conscious attempt to demean or threaten you, going through official channels is the right thing to do. Did you misunderstand the remark? Maybe a clarifying conversation is the right path. If the remark was made out of pure ignorance, a sincere conversation explaining why the remark was offensive might be the solution.

How you handle a potential conflict in the workplace can significantly impact careers and the organization as a whole. Sometimes a person has to go. Sometimes you have to call in HR, the lawyers, and the union reps. But sometimes, a discussion that educates, heals, and dispels fear can be far more advantageous than a forced apology or other punitive measures. When you can rise above the knee-jerk reaction, you demonstrate the poise and professionalism that higher positions require.

It may feel like you are a victim sometimes, but you still have a choice. No one can make you angry—you have to decide to be angry. The most effective response you can give is one that makes you look mature, professional, and in control of yourself. The short-term payoff of berating someone who did you wrong will result in remorse and a damaged reputation. Don't lower yourself; behave in a way that will serve your long-term interests.

Those that use workplace politics for their own ends can destroy an organization. When workplace politics takes hold and gets out of hand, one of the biggest problems it creates is diminishing trust. This is an extremely serious issue. The ripple effect can harm major aspects of the organization, such as the flow of information. When information is manipulated, altered, or suppressed, it becomes unreliable. When people can't trust information, they stop sharing it, and they stop helping each other. The organization's lifeblood stagnates, and the organization begins to atrophy.

Leaders must pay attention to and address any issues that might be brewing. The beauty of the servant leader model that we talked about is that employees will be far more likely to inform you of rumors, gossip, and other issues that might be brewing.

You will want to know the actual power structure in your organization as opposed to the one neatly laid out in an organizational chart. There will be natural leaders—some are loud and vocal; others might be quiet and say few words. While the person on the soapbox during lunch might attract a crowd, be aware of the quiet one in the corner that everyone seeks for advice and information. Identify assets and potential trouble in your organization by watching and listening. People joining and leaving the organization, or moving up the ladder, will affect this structure.

Most workplace politics begin with a personal quest for upward movement, basically, more money. But, sometimes, the motivations can be less clear. Some people just like to cause trouble. Sometimes politics are geared toward ruining a single person that an individual has taken a dislike to. Whatever the reason, it can get complicated to deal with, so it's always best to catch it early.

This brings me to office gossip. Office gossip isn't office politics; it's informal communication between employees. It may be negative or positive, trivial or important, but it will certainly be incomplete, inaccurate, and just plain wrong. But it's what your employees are saying when they feel safe and what they are hearing. Tap into that, but don't abuse it. It can be a source of information that can be put to good use. Find out about personal events and milestones that might have been overlooked. Or reports on bad employees or other complaints that people are too afraid to report or might think too trivial. Or rumors that can be put to rest quickly.

Don't try to suppress or control office gossip because you can't. You will simply be cut out of the loop if you betray a trust or act rashly on something you've heard. In addition, you need to be especially careful when dealing with some individuals that are experts in manipulation. They can hide behind others they've manipulated into acting for them through lies, flattery, intimidation, or even blackmail.

When dealing with office politics and gossip, you take a risk as it is all hearsay, anecdotal, and undocumented. Acting on, even inquiring about, certain information could get you in legal trouble. The key here is that you know what is being said in your organization, not that you need to act on it immediately. In some cases, you will want to consult legal counsel.

How do you avoid situations in your organization due to workplace politics? Remove the stiflers addressed in this book from your organization, and you will significantly diminish the chances of an ugly event occurring due to office politics. The best antidote for poisonous office politics is good leadership.

Start by demanding accountability from everyone in the organization and deal with those that engage in political behavior. Employees need to be comfortable. They need to trust you and feel trusted. Once people begin sowing confusion, doubt, and negativity of any form in the workplace, the damage spreads rapidly. People will go into self-preservation mode and lose trust in those around them.

Workplace politics will happen, and it is the responsibility of the leaders to accept that and deal with it effectively.

Sometimes a simple misunderstanding can turn political. People are so different that language can be interpreted differently.

A facial expression can be taken the wrong way, or a comment can be taken out of context. Past traumas can severely affect the way we perceive an event. It is common sense that when many humans interact, complex dynamics are created, and issues will arise. A silly comment or innocent to one person may be deeply offensive or even threatening to another. While the injured party may have a perfect poker face and even seem happy, they may be so deeply offended or threatened that they will take drastic action. Whether that's a legal action or a personal vendetta, it's always best to head off bad situations if you can.

Another solution to out-of-control politics at work is the develop and encourage positive activities where employees can bond. Create the opposite energy by deepening and developing trust, communication, and camaraderie. A softball or bowling team, trust retreat, or even the occasional company picnic can accomplish this. A company with engaged employees will see the organization as something to protect, as it protects them, rather than a giant mindless entity where it's every person for themselves.

Workplace politics occur in every company, large or small. When people aren't happy, they talk, and they sometimes take matters into their own hands. As a result, things can get divisive, performance suffers, and productivity drops.

*

Workplace politics can be nasty and problematic at all levels. Still, it must be managed, or things will only get worse in your career or organization. Remember to be clear about the difference between advancement dependent on unethical or illegal criteria and simply dealing with office politics. Most important, you should never tolerate any demeaning, unethical, or illegal treatment.

CHAPTER FOURTEEN

Training

"The only thing worse than training your employees and having them leave is not training them and having them stay."

—Henry Ford

POOR OR INADEQUATE TRAINING CAN HAVE myriad negative effects, from unsafe working conditions, legal issues, reduced productivity, and increased turnover to customer dissatisfaction. Training is critical. The price of not properly training people is far more significant than the cost of the training. Employees are an investment and not an expense.

A prime example of this approach is KitchenAid. They hire workers based on their willingness to work; then they provide them with six weeks of training. KitchenAid takes a long-term approach and invests in people to make sure they have the hard skills to do their job. Intangibles like work ethic and raw ability transcend the labels of race, gender, and the like and are almost impossible to teach. KitchenAid knows that it is easier to teach the hard skills a person needs to work for them than these intangible soft skills.

So, where do you start? There are two areas of training that need to be addressed. First, what are the areas in which training needs to occur? And second, what are the different ways to train people?

I like to reinforce any training that was recently received. After a training session, we tend to get back to our job and slide right back into the old way of doing things. I like to utilize the training immediately if at all possible. At the very least, I will review all my notes and make sure I have a solid grasp of what I learned.

Since employees are often asked to evaluate any training they undergo, I thought it would be helpful to mention the Kirkpatrick Model.[23] This is a globally recognized method used to evaluate training or learning systems. This method uses four measures to rate the training: reaction, learning, behavior, and results. I have used it and find it easier to write up any required evaluation, especially if you are familiar with it beforehand.

First, I look at the reaction I had to the training. Was it interesting? Did the instructor inspire confidence and keep me engaged? How did I feel about the training? Then I consider what I learned. Do I feel like I got the information or skills I need? Was it up-to-date and relevant? Then there's the aftermath. Did the training cause me to see things differently or change me in a way that was intended? Can I apply the knowledge and skills I just absorbed? The results are the last thing I consider. Can I measure the effectiveness of the training in hard data? Am I getting higher sales numbers, fewer accidents, fewer complaints, or better performance? If you take weapons training and walk away afraid of your weapon and making fewer bulls-eyes, that's a problem.

So, what are the different ways you can train an employee? Whether you are starting a career and want to assess the seriousness and effectiveness of the training you might receive or in management and tasked with developing the training, it would

[23] "The Kirkpatrick Model," Kirkpatrick Partners, accessed September 16, 2021, https://www.kirkpatrickpartners.com/Our-Philosophy/The-Kirkpatrick-Model.

be useful to know your options. Using the wrong method for training can be tedious or even counterproductive.

Let's start with the most common ways employees are trained.

Hands-on, or on-the-job training, is self-explanatory. For example, most of us have had a minimum wage job where we were immediately put to work doing simple, often physical tasks; then we gradually learned the more complex systems and skills involved. Using this method, the employee is immediately productive for the organization.

By using this method, you risk impeded production, mistakes, and possible losses or accidents. Therefore, this method is best used for simple tasks and jobs.

A similar method to hands-on is the closed environment, or limited open, exercise. Employees perform their job for other employees and specific guests to learn by doing. Without "real" customers to serve, more time can be spent helping the trainees develop. This approach is similar to role-playing, where employees perform various aspects of their jobs, especially workplace and customer interaction.

Having a mentor or more experienced partner at work can be very effective. There is no substitute for a person that knows the job, culture, and industry for learning the ropes.

Sometimes more traditional ways of learning are unavoidable, such as classroom lectures and presentations. However, there is no replacement for coming together for specific interactions. Discussions, role-play, and very focused training can often be best accomplished in small work groups. The participants in these training groups often bond and become supports for each other long after the training is complete.

When you need to disseminate information to a large group of people, you might want to default to these methods, but don't forget there are other technological solutions. To be sure that employees are reviewing and understanding the material, develop online quizzes and questionnaires to test their knowledge.

When the material is complex, you might need an instructor to present it and answer questions and clarify information. It is unnecessary to host a traditional in-person classroom experience. Now we have online options for e-learning where the participants can be anywhere in the world. This can reduce the time and monetary costs associated with traditional classroom learning.

Another growing trend since technology has become more commonplace, affordable, and acceptable by most individuals is simulations. These can be anything from a simulated interaction where multiple-choice questions and answers test and score the employee on their knowledge and decision-making to full virtual reality experiences such as aircraft simulators for pilots and mannequins for nurses and physicians.

Airline pilots have long used flight simulators that allow for realistic training in situations that would be extremely dangerous, prohibitively expensive, or simply impossible to experience otherwise. The most advanced simulators used by the military and commercial airlines can cost several million dollars. These simulators are exact duplicates of real cockpits and include the functioning instruments and mechanisms. The entire cockpit moves on massive hydraulics, the sounds and lighting conditions are reproduced, and outside the windows is a view of what the pilot would actually see. Although these simulators are costly to build and maintain, an instructor can create a simulation for a pilot where they must attempt to land a commercial airliner with one engine on fire, at night, with no instruments or landing gear. The cost of a simulator that allows for this level of training more than pays for itself. There is no way to calculate how many disasters have been averted and lives have been saved by well-trained pilots around the world.

You also need to determine what they are being trained for? What requires that an employee be trained and to what level of expertise? Here are common areas where training is often used in organizations.

Basic orientation. Like many of us had when we attended college, many organizations have an orientation. Here newcomers are instructed on the organization's culture, mission, values, goals, policies, and laws. They may include a tour of the premises, a map, informational materials, and being told where to get resources and assistance. During orientation, there may be a presentation by various departments and individuals. In addition, company rules, policies, and regulations might be reviewed.

Orientation can be a few hours or a few days, depending on the organization's size. A highly regulated industry might have many laws and procedures to go over. In this case, the line between orientation and training might be blurred.

Skills development might take place immediately or on an as-needed basis. Some jobs require constant training, qualifying, and requalifying. Law enforcement agencies, for example, require monthly weapons practice and yearly recertification. There is an increasing number of required seminars and certificates for police officers, such as CPR, forensics, sensitivity training, and education on specific specialties. Salespeople are often trained on the products they sell.

In general, the more technical or dangerous your job, the more responsibility you are trusted with, the more frequent and intense your training will be. Some industries move so rapidly that training and education are a constant.

There is also training for soft skills such as communication and problem-solving. Some jobs will require immediate training in core soft skills that are important to the job, like patient interaction, negotiation, communications, and presentations. Sometimes an employee is selected for further training due to a deficit or because they are being prepared for advancement. Individual improvement skills can be for personal aspects such as anger management, teamwork, and public speaking. There can also be advanced training in conflict resolution, leadership, and crisis management.

Training also extends to products, services and can be quite involved. A salesperson can be educated on all the options, functions, pros, and cons of a product. Even field technicians are often educated to be good ambassadors of a brand or product. People often trust the person in overalls installing a product more than the sharply dressed person with the agenda to sell. An organization will benefit from having employees from every level step into as many other roles as possible. Working in the trenches can give management information and insight they would never gain otherwise. Understanding the high-level mission and goals of the organization can make people feel respected and invested.

And there's quality and safety training. Ensuring that products are assembled, tested, packaged correctly will minimize returns, complaints, and possible legal situations. Ensuring customer satisfaction is important, as well as obeying any laws and regulations you must follow.

Safety training can be as simple as instructing people on preventing an injury, where the fire extinguishers are, and how to evacuate the building. Or, depending on the industry, it could be a very involved and lengthy process. Recently, safety training has expanded to include workplace violence, active shooters, and bomb threats.

In several industries, safety training is a huge part of the job. For example, handling dangerous materials, search and rescue, ER staff, and large construction projects will require a massive amount of time and effort to train for and uphold safety.

Training at all levels can be critical. Even seminars on workplace sensitivity, which some may view as a waste of time, can be looked at as an opportunity for growth or simply as a tool to prevent expensive legal and PR issues. However you view it, training at all levels is essential for a wide variety of reasons.

*

On the one hand, training can be an area where a lot of time and money is wasted, but on the other, not nearly enough time and money is allocated toward it. In addition, poor or inadequate training can create issues that range from minor to severe—from increased turnover to organizational destruction. Therefore, training is critical, and the price of not training people properly can be worse than just stifling your organization.

Training employees is an investment and not an expense.

CHAPTER FIFTEEN

Managing Leadership Transitions In The Workplace

"The greatest danger in times of turbulence is not the turbulence—it is to act with yesterday's logic."

—Peter Drucker

FOR THE MOST PART, CHANGE OR transition in the workplace makes many people insecure or left with many questions. They wonder if the change is for the better, if promises made will be kept, and how the changes will affect them. More than ever, it is critical that we know how to manage change as it is happening at an unprecedented pace. Already there has been a massive amount of change thrust upon us in the last year. We are seeing many people changing jobs, starting new positions, and even embarking on new careers. Handling change is challenging enough, but the sheer number of changes makes the task even more daunting. Add to this all the latest changes to the workplace, and you have an overwhelming amount of challenge on your hands.

There are a few primary areas you can focus on that will make a transition smoother for everyone involved. In the book *Leading Organizations: Ten Timeless Truths,* Scott Keller and Mary Meaney list ten fundamental issues that leaders face during a transition. The truths are attracting and retaining talent, developing current talent, managing performance, creating leadership teams, decision-making, reorganizing to capture value quickly, reducing long-term overhead costs, making culture a competitive advantage, leading transformational change, and transitioning to new leadership roles.[24]

The authors arrived at this list by taking "stock of the most common questions their clients ask them in the areas of human capital, organization design, transformational change, and merger management." This is a useful list and a good starting point to discuss why transitions in the workplace are essential, especially changes in leadership and management.

A change in leadership at a company is one of the most volatile times a member of the organization will experience. The way these transitions are handled by the outgoing, incoming, and remaining leaders is crucial. Everyone is looking to these individuals to determine how they should be processing the changes. All communications, conscious and unconscious, are picked up on by people affected. The changes impact many people's careers, investments, and futures. Sadly, most leaders are not prepared for these changes and don't realize the impact their words and actions have on those around them.

In *Leading Organizations,* life's biggest challenges are ranked in order of difficulty, and number one on the list is transitioning at work. This is ahead of grief, divorce, and health issues. This is not

---

[24] Scott Keller and Mary Meaney, *Leading Organizations: Ten Timeless Truths* (London: Bloomsbury, 2017).

surprising as the success, or failure, of the company and all those dependent on it, is tied to the leader.

According to the book, nine times out of ten, a successful transition translates into a successful future for the company and all involved. Successful transitions translate into lower attrition rates and higher revenue and profits. Conversely, they also noted that unsuccessful transitions lead to lower performance and higher attrition rates. This was taken from a report by McKinsey & Company, Successfully Transitioning to New Leadership Roles, May 23, 2018.[25] It's clear that a successful leader will likely lead to a successful company, but what we are specifically talking about is the transition before any actual proof of success or failure has been presented. This transitional time is critical in determining whether the leader will be successful. Overlooking the importance of this process is why nearly half of transitions fail to some degree. There is a broad definition of what constitutes a failure but having rates that range from 25 percent to nearly 50 percent is arguably too high. Fortunately, much can be done to lower this high rate of failure.

Let's look at what is most often cited as the main issue: organizational politics. Nearly 70 percent of transitions see trouble immediately based on the failure to manage workplace politics, culture, and individual issues. Most leaders express regret at not having handled these issues immediately.

These successful people are getting tripped up because they fail to realize or accept just how critical this process is. Marshall Goldsmith said, "What got you here won't get you there." This has never been more appropriate than in a transition of management.

As frequent as leadership transitions are, few leaders get help when they occur. With the increased change, these transitions occur in most organizations, and many happen simultaneously.

---

[25] Scott Keller and Mary Meaney, "Successfully Transitioning to New Leadership Roles," *McKinsey Quarterly*, January 12, 2018, https://www.mckinsey.com/business-functions/organization/our-insights/successfully-transitioning-to-new-leadership-roles.

New departments are being formed while old ones are being phased out. Many people are hired to work in jobs they've never done before. These are often jobs that didn't exist a few months ago or not in such great numbers as they do now. Few organizations have training in place for these positions, experienced staff to do the training, or the time to dedicate to training.

In addition to the pandemic, the pace of change has constantly been rising over the past few decades. The turnover rate for a CEO has jumped from about 12 percent in 2010 to about 17 percent in 2015. When a new manager comes in, many people lose their jobs, quit, or are moved to another position. Up to 70 percent of all people under a new manager can expect there to be a dramatic change in their workplace. That's a lot of uncertainty to deal with and a massive stifler to an organization.

Besides all the changes, there is cost. A transition costs money and time. There are fees paid to executive search firms, recruiters, and applicable job sites. Flying a potential hire out, putting them up in a hotel, and entertaining them can get costly. New furniture, renovations, relocations, and other physical costs can accrue. There are bonuses paid out, severance packages, and other adjustments to the payroll. This cost has been estimated to be over 200 percent of their annual salary for a senior executive. But the highest cost is all the time this takes. As your organization engages in the business of finding a new leader—a process that might take a year or more—the market continues to evolve, and the competition continues to engage in its business.

Yet, many transitions are not handled well. People are dropped into new positions largely unprepared, and those under the new leader are clueless about what is about to happen to them and their careers. Here are a few things to do before, during, and after a transition. First, be clear on what will happen and because of the transition.

"To be prepared is half the victory," said Miguel de Cervantes, and you prepare by asking questions. For a transition, it's essential to know about the incoming leader, the organization's culture, how the team will be impacted, and other areas that should be brainstormed and recorded so they can be addressed.

In 2013, the CEO of Netflix sent a memo detailing a new commitment to expand its mission from only distributing digital content to become producers of that content. He was committed to funding the production of original content, the kind that would win awards. Since that memo, Netflix has almost tripled its revenue, its profits have multiplied by a factor of thirty-two, and its stock has increased in value annually.

This means you need to be driven by the impact of the transition and not strictly by a schedule. It might take longer than the typical 100-day window. One hundred days is a guideline, not a deadline. There is no hard data to support this notion, but there is evidence that a rushed or poorly executed transition will fail. Significantly changing an organization of almost any size can be complex, and timetables need to remain flexible.

If you are the new leader, you can do a few things to ensure a transition goes smoothly. First, spend adequate time understanding who you are taking over for. Determine what they did right. Don't plan to sweep everything away when you enter the picture. Keep things in place that are successful or benign to help maintain a sense of stability for employees. Know the organization you are stepping into. Get to know the unwritten things as well as the documented processes and numbers. Talk to the employees. Get the real scoop on things and make sure the people know who this new person is coming in to take over. Involve people in the transition. This goes for important clients and vendors too. Invest all important stakeholders in the transition. Make them feel empowered and not victimized.

Build an environment where everyone feels involved in the transition and is an integral part of the process. This act alone will increase retention significantly. Include them in the plans and make sure they can authentically assist in the transformation process. This must be genuine; people can tell when they are being patronized, which can be worse than doing nothing. And don't forget to include discussions about company culture and traditions. If the transition is a merger, the culture must merge too, or people will feel left out.

Although you want to take as much time as it requires for the process to be accomplished correctly, you need to implement the transition plan quickly. Times during transitions are generally less productive times for the organization, so you want to minimize the time the process takes.

Finally, monitor the progress of the transition. A new leader is like an organ transplant for an organization, and you want to do everything you can to ensure the new heart of the organization isn't rejected. This needs to be done regularly for months, even after the company is fully functioning. Walk or travel around and get face-to-face with your organization. Having informal meetings with managers and team leads can be very telling. I say informal because you want to get an unvarnished view. In fact, this type of clean-slate process is a golden opportunity to implement much of what is discussed in this book.

I have seen many organizations where a new CEO comes in, consults with almost no one, makes sweeping changes, and turns up the stifle meter to "high." Barging into a new environment blind, expecting to wield your authority to get things done is a huge mistake. You can destroy a lot before you even get started as people quickly realize they don't matter, and their days might be numbered. They shut down, look for other jobs, and the situation will only get worse as time passes. You have less of a grip on the situation instead of getting a tighter grip you had hoped for.

Once you are settling in as a new leader, despite your best efforts, there will be challenges. The best you can hope for is to reduce the challenges and diminish the negative impact of those you can't. Here is a quick bullet list to consider.

- Be aware that every person is affected by the change.
- Be transparent and accessible.
- Solicit and acknowledge ideas from the staff.
- Encourage new and existing people's interaction.

- Be very clear on what you expect.
- Understand the leader that is leaving and don't badmouth them.

When talking to the outgoing manager, which is not always a possibility, keep these conversation points in mind. Ask about the employees and their strengths and weaknesses. Discover the ambitions of the high performers and facilitate them. Get information on the organization as a whole. If the transition is acrimonious, you might need to take it all with a grain of salt. But even if the transition is positive, you will want to verify what you can. The outgoing manager's input can be valuable but possibly misleading if you aren't careful. I find it very useful to ask for the resumes of those who will be directly reporting to me as well as the most recent performance reviews. It shocks me how many new leaders come into an organization and take almost no time to get to know the backgrounds of the people working for them.

Most important is to build trust with the new team immediately. Introduce yourself, mingle with them, make sure they know that you care about them, and be available to them. When in conversation, ask the person about themselves. Ask about their time at the company and what they think of the changes. Ask them to tell you how the transition feels to them. Ask them to talk about their department and their work and what they would like to see improved. Finally, ask them what would make their job more comfortable. And act. If you are at an informal function, facilitate some way so you will not forget to follow up on the discussions you had. A follow-up on a casual conversation is a powerful way to win people over.

Remember that the existing employees hold valuable knowledge. A new leader is often brought in to make changes, but not everything needs to be changed. Don't throw out or overlook that replacing and retraining new people to do a task takes a lot of time and money. Also, never forget that often people will tell you, the new leader, what they want you to believe and not necessarily what you need to know. I once came into a company, and one of my direct reports, a VP, told me three of his staff were terrible and needed to go, and the other three were stars. Guess what? Nearly the opposite was the truth. Two of the "stars" were "yes men" who didn't rock the boat; the "terrible three" were pushing back at a lot of the VP's nonsense. Over time, "terrible three" became the high performing stars under a new VP.

You are there to make organizational changes, but your number one job is to manage people. Do it right, and substantial positive changes will occur.

*

Remember that every workplace transition will make most people insecure, and they will have a lot of questions. Be prepared to explain how the changes are for the better and remind them of the promises that were made and how they are being actively fulfilled.

This chapter is particularly important as managing change is now more important than ever. Already there has been a massive amount of change thrust upon us in the last year. People are changing jobs, starting new positions, and even embarking on new careers. Handling change is challenging enough, but the sheer number of changes makes the task even more daunting. Add to this all the new and unknown changes to the workplace, and you have a very real challenge on your hands.

CHAPTER SIXTEEN

Managing The Modern Workplace

> "If you are working on something exciting that you really care about, you don't have to be pushed. The vision pulls you."
>
> —Steve Jobs

LEADING AND MANAGING IN THE COMING years will be radically different from the past. Things are already very different between the pandemic, rapidly evolving technology, and the newer generation of workers. There will be many challenges, and challenges always bring opportunities. Let's look at some of the most important things we can do as leaders and managers to adapt to and benefit from these major workplace changes.

Psychological Safety

First, let's look at the notion of the "safe space." People need a safe space to experiment, fail, and ultimately learn. And the modern world, with its increasingly invasive and overwhelming technology, almost demands that we have a safe space to go to—a place where we can unplug and gather our thoughts. The idea of a safe space comes from psychological safety. An article in August 2017 by Laura Delizonna in the *Harvard Business Review* summed it up. "The highest performing teams have one thing in common: psychological safety, the belief that you won't be punished when you make a mistake. Studies show that psychological safety allows for moderate risk-taking, speaking your mind, creativity, and sticking your neck out without the fear of having your head cut off."[26] Coincidentally, these are just the types of behavior that lead to market breakthroughs. So how can you increase your psychological safety on your team? First, approach conflicts as a collaborator, not as an adversary.

When conflicts arise, use a learning mindset where you're curious to hear the other person's viewpoint. Listen and ask for clarifying feedback to be sure you understand. Once you create a sense of psychological safety on your team, you can expect to see higher levels of engagement, increased motivation to tackle difficult problems, more learning and development opportunities, and better performance.

There's also a quote in the article from a person at Google. "There's no team without trust." Google did a two-year study on team performance which revealed that "The highest performing teams have one thing in common, and that thing is psychological safety. The belief that you won't be punished when you make a mistake."

Psychological safety is something that we must be sensitive to and cognizant of. It's an ever-evolving process. There will always be people afraid of being ostracized or punished for speaking their mind and those that won't stop speaking their minds. It takes the whole organization to implement and maintain these cultural practices. They must start at the top and work their way down.

---

[26] Laura Delizonna, "High-Performing Teams Need Psychological Safety. Here's How to Create It," *Harvard Business Review*, August 24, 2017, https://hbr.org/2017/08/high-performing-teams-need-psychological-safety-heres-how-to-create-it.

It's something that organizations have to aspire to and create an environment where people can speak up without the fear of retribution.

Managers need to understand that they will get much higher levels of engagement when they embrace an environment that isn't punitive or retaliatory. I know from experience as my last US corporate organization that I managed had high engagement scores. It was due to a comprehensive cultural practice. When you have high engagement, you usually have high productivity and much lower turnover.

Most leaders nowadays are very open to learning, adopting new behaviors, and a new culture in a company. There are times when it's forced, and that never works; it has to be an authentic effort. Being authentic can be straightforward. For me, it means being open, honest, and ethical. Leaders need to be vulnerable in that sense. But most important, and this is the thing that most leaders struggle with, is knowing what they don't know. In an article about his book, *Hot Seat* in *Corporate Board Member* magazine, Jeff Immelt, the former Chair and CEO of GE, is quoted, "In certain moments, the right answer would have been for me to say, I don't know."

Early in my career, I was fileted and sauteed by a general manager who lit into me (in private) about telling the division president that, "I did not know." The GM told me to lie or make something up but to *never* say "I don't know." That was at the end of the day, and I went home and thought about it. The next day, I went into my boss's office, who reported to the GM and told him, the president of the division is smart enough to know everyone cannot know everything. Don't get me wrong, there are things you damn well better know when you are running a business and things you cannot be expected to know, and you need to know the difference.

Being vulnerable isn't being weak.

People in upper management are often lulled into a sense of, "I'm the boss and must know everything." Or at least they loathe the idea of being less knowledgeable or informed than their employees, so they can't admit they don't know everything. Managers often believe they must make all the right decisions and cannot be seen as ignorant or weak. Leaders fail because they don't know what they don't know or won't admit what they don't know.

With the pace and complexity of the world today, you have to rely on other people; you can't pretend you don't need other people anymore. You need to assess your strengths and weaknesses accurately. It's impossible to know the answer to everything. And leaders who can't admit that will seem less than authentic and worse, will fail.

So, how does a type A personality let themselves be vulnerable? How do you transition from know-it-all authority to being more authentic? First, know that being vulnerable doesn't mean being weak or irresponsible. The idea isn't to expose yourself to harm or negativity. As a leader, you can't be vulnerable all the time. There is a distinction here. Being vulnerable is occasionally showing that you are human and have feelings.

John Maxwell said, "People don't care how much you know until they know how much you care." People show up to work every day, and a lot of what happens outside of work affects them. Are their parents sick? Did a pet die? Is a close relative going through a divorce? Did they get in a car accident? Can they pay their bills? We too often look at other people and assume they only exist in the work environment. We all need to remember that other people have lives, issues, and challenges. We need to understand that we are whole persons—not just one at work and another at home.

To make this approach organization-wide, like most things, you need to start at the top. How leaders react and respond sets the tone of the entire organization. If the people at the top don't care, very few below them will. Culture flows downhill.

Another aspect of establishing a psychologically safe workspace is to set up an environment where debate can happen, dialogue can occur, and tough questions can be asked with no repercussions. I spent eleven years at Abbott Laboratories, from

1989 to 2000, and our financial planning cycle was three cycles long. It took up the vast majority of the year. Those were very tough sessions. People had to understand the drivers of what they were managing, whether it was the costs in the manufacturing facility, employee benefits, regulatory work, sales, marketing, or finance. You had to understand the business, and there were lots of questions. There were lots of challenges. And there were three layers of each review.

First, you had a review with the vice president over your area; then there was a review with the division president. Finally, there was a review with the chief operating officer. And this happened three times a year.

Tom Hudson, the COO for the vast majority of my time at Abbott, was an incredibly brilliant, bright, detail-oriented, and phenomenal businessperson; above all, he was fair. He knew a lot about our business, and he knew the right questions to ask. We got into some fairly heated debates, but being challenged is an important part of running and managing a business. We need to teach the people the difference between argument and debate, safety and isolation, and other important distinctions.

In a Harvard Business Review article entitled "Connect, Then Lead," authors Amy Cuddy, Matthew Kohut, and John Neffinger share what many leaders intuitively know to be true. Leaders who can establish a meaningful connection with employees will ultimately exert greater influence than those who can't.[27]

You can start building those connections immediately. I go back to the John Maxwell phrase, again. "People don't care how much you know until they know how much you care." Particularly now, postpandemic, showing your team how much you care is essential. Most important, I believe, is understanding that your people have a life outside of work. Understanding

[27] Amy J.C. Cuddy, Matthew Kohut, and John Neffinger, "Connect, Then Lead," *Harvard Business Review,* July-August 2013, https://hbr.org/2013/07/connect-then-lead.

nonwork pressures is simply critical. I have a story I love to share that addresses this.

A former CEO of a successful health care company was sitting on the board of a nonhealth-related public company. He was asked to take over for the CEO who was out with a health issue. One of the first things they did was give everybody on their staff a significant slug of stock in the company, worth a million dollars. Then he said to his staff, "One of the most derailing things in a person's life is financial travails. Now, you are all millionaires, so let's get to work."

That's powerful! Equity-based incentives are there to help drive value for the company, but they also put the recipients in stable situations financially in many instances, so they are truly focused on work. They're there for a purpose—to reward—and create an environment where people feel comfortable and do the right thing for the business.

But it's not just about giving large gifts to people. Even the smallest thoughts and gestures can have huge rewards. Making sure that people get breaks to refresh their minds and get the blood moving is essential for health and productivity. When people spend all day on back-to-back Zoom meetings, they might not move enough. CNN medical reporter and neurosurgeon Sanjay Gupta said, "Sitting is the new smoking of our generation." That might be an overstatement, but not by much. The meeting leader needs to make sure people get up and move around. Self-care is really important.

I still try to take as many calls on my phone as I do on Zoom using video. I just tell people I'm old school and I like to use the telephone. I do an extensive amount of executive coaching and mentoring now and have international clients in many industries. Some executive coaches are adamant that video distracts from the coaching process because people are more concerned about how they look. Some coaches refuse to use Zoom with video because they think it hurts their ability to coach. But I agree; coaching needs to have focus, and you have to be mentally present. Zoom with video on is visual; it can be distracting.

Like authenticity, inspiration comes from the heart. It's not going to happen using a program, a project, or from a speech by a motivational speaker. Inspiring people is like making a roux. A roux is made by melting butter or fat over medium-low heat and adding an equal amount of flour. You stir this constantly and, in a few minutes, you have a slightly thick, light sauce (roux). The roux is the basis of many recipes. And there are only two ingredients.

But here's the trick. Just because you have those two simple ingredients doesn't mean you can make a roux. There's an art to it and some science. It's not enough to have the right ingredients; you have to know all the subtleties of heat, timing, motion, and numerous small variables, which determine whether you make a roux or a mess. Inspiring people is the same. It's not just a list of what to do; you must be genuine in your approach and desire.

The power of caring.

One of the things I've found in my experience is that there's no substitute for showing people you want to help them develop. Helping people learn and grow is inspirational. The most important questions to ask people when trying to help them grow is, "How do you want to grow? What are you interested in doing?" When I ran my last company, I told people that the most important thing is to do what you love. After a speech at a national sales meeting, one of the sales reps said, "Jim, I really don't want to be a sales rep. It's not my passion. I want to be a teacher." So, I told him, "That's great. It's important you realized that. Don't quit your job. Keep doing what you're doing until you get a teaching job." About nine months later, he sent me an email thanking me.

Speaking of safe spaces, I'd be willing to bet a lot of money that if most people told a senior leader in an organization they didn't want to be in their job, they would be fired.

An administrative assistant for a senior executive at Abbott Laboratories wanted to go out and sell. I don't think she'd ever sold anything in her life, but the company helped her get out into the field. She became a powerful salesperson.

No one can help you develop you until they understand what you want to do. There is on-the-job training for skills in Excel, Word, and PowerPoint but it's the intersection of your skills/expertise, your passion, and where others see value in you. Finding a job at the intersection of these three things (what some refer to as "the sweet spot") will propel you forward. Generally, personal development and growth are critical as there are fewer opportunities for advancement.

Robert L. Parkinson, who retired as a board member and chief operating officer at Abbott, went on to be the Dean of Loyola University of Chicago (his alma mater), and chairman and CEO of Baxter International. I first met Bob in 1985, four years before I joined Abbott Laboratories. Bob became a good friend, confidant, and mentor. You knew that when you were with Bob, he was focused on you. He didn't look around; he didn't look at his phone or his computer. He sat with you at a conference table, not behind his desk, and made everything about you. When you had a conversation with him, he'd ask questions and then repeat what you said to clarify that he understood what you were saying. This was how he demonstrated that he was listening intently to what you were saying. I always thought that was absolutely fabulous.

I am not nearly as successful at this as he was; it was second nature to him. I try not to be distracted, but I've got terrible ADHD, so distractions are powerful. To deal with my ADHD, I've been open about it. I mentioned earlier in the book that in my last big job, I told my staff that if I got distracted to call a time out. Soliciting people for help is fair. I don't want to waste people's time going down some sidebar conversation that isn't important to what we're talking about. It isn't a good use of people's time and energy.

Another important thing when it comes to inspiration is making sure that people know that what they are doing is essential to the organization. I don't think there's any substitute for this. For those of us in the medical and health care fields, we're fortunate that we can bring patients in to tell our story. When someone whose life was saved because of a product you are selling, that's powerful.

In my forty years in health care, there's nothing more compelling than having a customer come in and tell you the products you made saved their life. It is very motivating to know that your products are having a dramatic impact on people's lives.

Making sure people understand what they're doing is important. Managers are obligated to help people understand this. And part of doing this is to get employee feedback. It's not critical that you get feedback from everybody all the time. Walmart's got a million employees, and they could spend billions of dollars just getting opinions. There are limits to this, and it's a judgment call by the leaders of the organization.

But with technology, there are a plethora of ways to get feedback from people. We've come a long way from the suggestion box. From new employee surveys, engagement surveys, anonymous surveys, pulse surveys, and exit interviews, we can quickly gather and process all this data. You can give incentives for participating, like drawings for cash, stock, and other perks. Many companies have online chat rooms, forums, discussion groups, and areas where people can vent. Many organizations have online town halls where people can comment and ask questions. And there are independent sites like Glassdoor where you can check out organizations and see what people are saying about them.

For example, in the world of selling medical devices, there are typically conventions and trade shows where our sales and marketing people spend hours on their feet at the booths and other events. They are demonstrating their products to the attendees, typically clinicians such as nurses and physicians. These are clinicians who have dedicated their time to come for personal education or credits for continuing education. As a senior leader of our US organization, I was always in the booths, standing with our people. I knew that my peers at the other major companies did not do this as I could see they were not in their booths. I wasn't there to sell! I was there to show the salespeople that I was no better than they were. Actions speak louder than words and show people you support them.

There is no substitute for walking the walk, showing people that you care, and that you support them by being right there with them.

Avoid the blame game.

When you have an after-action review (AAR) or a postmortem after an event, you must create an environment where people don't personalize the process. Honest and accurate evaluation is critical to improvement. This goes back to having a psychologically safe environment. Questions need to be asked, like, "What could have gone better? What can we learn from our mistakes?" You never want to punish people for honest mistakes and shortcomings. This will signal the entire organization that you better not screw up or there will be dire consequences.

Once, the chairman of a company I worked with went to see an important partner in Asia. There was a discussion as to whether or not the CEOs of these two companies should exchange gifts. We received a clear message that there would be no gift exchange, but when our CEO arrived, the other CEO gave him a gift. The person responsible for setting up that meeting, a vice president level executive, was demoted almost immediately after the meeting. When things like that happen, they go viral in an organization quickly. Then people are reticent and very fearful of making any mistake. This, in turn, kills creativity, innovation, and advancement. Stopping this starts at the top if, of course, the top so chooses.

Avoiding the blame game and other toxic behaviors is critical. When people are afraid to speak up, mistakes can happen. Sometimes those mistakes can be fatal or at the very least, costly. That's why having these open and honest checks and balances in place is critical.

Atul Gawande wrote the book *The Checklist Manifesto.* It's about how operating room staff can ensure that mistakes are less likely by making sure the teams involved in key decisions are part of a system of checks and balances. This is particularly important in mission-critical fields like medicine or wherever fatigue can be a factor.

Machines wear out, parts aren't 100 percent perfect, and things can deteriorate from there. The likelihood of accidents and mistakes increases. When something looks a little aberrant, messages must go up the chain and not be quashed.

Good leaders set expectations and standards. They don't want surprises, and the only way to avoid them is by making sure people feel safe and not hesitant to speak up. It's especially critical these days as things have become very complex and sophisticated.

Avoid negativity at all costs.

Remember that you and other people have bad days. There are many things outside of the workplace and outside our control. But keep in mind that you can control your thoughts and reactions. My children used to come home from school complaining about their teachers. They might say, "Mrs. Jones did this," or "Mr. Jones did that." I'd stop them and remind them there are two things they need to know. First, in ten years, they won't remember this day and what happened. Second, Mr. Jones didn't ruin their day; *they* ruined their day. I'd remind them that they were in control of their day, not the teacher. People need to understand that. You control your thoughts and actions.

There are many reasons people act poorly. People have a lot of stuff going on in their lives, just like you do, and it almost always has nothing to do with you. It may be something very personal, private, or embarrassing. You can't read their minds, and it's none of your business. But if someone who is generally positive is acting poorly, you need to get a sense of what's happening and what you as a manager might need to do about it.

We see many struggles in our organizations that need addressing. Still, when conversations take place outside of the mission, vision, and values of the organization, you need to take heed. When people talk about things like politics, a potential firestorm of anger and hurt feelings can erupt and become a huge distraction. In some companies, CEOs are condoning those conversations, and in others, they are shutting them down. It's up to every leader to decide where they are on that issue, but it needs to be acknowledged and managed. There's a balance to be reached. You may vote for whomever you want. I just don't want you to bring that political conversation into the organization because that's not why we're here. We're not running a political campaign. We're making medical devices to save people's lives. There's plenty of opportunities for you to volunteer, give money, and help support your candidate outside of work. But right here, right now, we're focused on company issues and not what we're struggling with as a country.

And yes, I understand the interrelationships. This doesn't include diversity, equity, or inclusion. They are very relevant, but don't get sidetracked by issues that should remain outside the organization.

*

Leadership and management practices have always been in flux, but recently we've seen massive changes in society and technology that have greatly amplified this trend. In the coming years, leaders and managers must remain sensitive to increasing diversity in the workplace, rapidly evolving technology, and newer generations of workers coming in after them. There will be many challenges, and challenges always bring opportunities.

CHAPTER SEVENTEEN

Management Postpandemic

"There will be interruptions, and I don't know when they will occur, and I don't how deep they will occur, I do know they will occur from time to time, and I also know that we'll come out better on the other end."

—Warren Buffet

THERE'S NO DENYING THAT THE PANDEMIC has dramatically impacted all of us and in so many ways. Virtually every person around the globe has been affected. Whether a change in work environments, management, culture, or society, our organizations will never be the same.

Sadly, in some cases, people lost their life savings paying bills. Some lost companies they'd built from the ground up as they were stressed to the point of shutting down. Some lost their homes, their mental health, and even their lives. It was devastating for many people.

But the pandemic has had a few good things come from it. For one, it has highlighted a key strength successful leaders call learning agility. Learning agility is not one skill but a collection of skills that allow people to learn new things and then apply what they've learned in another place. The ability to learn, adapt, unlearn, and relearn while keeping up with a perpetually changing world is learning agility. Leaders with learning agility will use this pandemic experience to become more powerful, more successful moving forward.

We've already seen companies pivot and do things they had no idea they were capable of doing. There are numerous stories, whether it was a hospital responding to the influx of patients or companies responding to the need for social distancing and touchless operations. Several companies put babysitting services in place, for example, so employees could work and not worry about childcare. There are staggering statistics about the number of patients that used telemedicine, as they were not able to visit a physician's office.

McKinsey reported that in early 2020, fewer than 1 percent of Medicare visits were done remotely; just a few months later, almost 50 percent were done online. Large hospital systems like Ascension Health System and the Cleveland Clinic saw their telemedicine go from thousands to millions in a very short time. Some of these numbers will decline as in-person visits are once again available. But many people won't want to leave the comfort of their home and travel or sit in a waiting room to talk to a professional. Why take two or more hours out of your day to talk to a person for twenty minutes when you can do it online? There are so many lessons from this pandemic that will forever change the way companies operate, the way people work, and how we manage going forward. Organizations have become much leaner by necessity. There's much more empowerment and transparency.

This pandemic pushed us to a point where doing nothing became riskier than doing something. People were compelled to do things, and many organizations that traditionally functioned from a command-and-control standpoint were suddenly faced with having to let the reins go and trust their people. The old way of doing things, "I'm the boss, and you are going to do what I tell you to do," is over. Leaders quickly found themselves relying on their people or failing. Many discovered that they had the capacity and capability to do many things. Ford Motor Company cranked out 2.5 million face shields in a matter of weeks. Companies with very little knowledge of making ventilators, for example, became ventilator manufacturers virtually overnight. Many amazing stories are coming out and will continue to come out of this pandemic experience.

All the data I've seen shows that people worked as hard, if not harder, and longer during the pandemic. One of the troubles created was that people didn't know when to disconnect, unplug, and stop working. Everything became focused on our computers, laptops, and other avenues of connectivity, and work surrounded us 24/7 if we weren't careful. Zoom offered ideas on how to manage Zoom fatigue. It highlighted more than ever how important it is to take breaks and not let people burn themselves out. People have to get up; they've got to move around. It took specific tactics by organizations to say, look, we've got to create gaps. How many times were you on a Zoom call where you had to run because the next Zoom was starting? We've got to provide gaps and spaces; people need to move around and be mobile. I will talk more about the tremendous mental stress we were all under at one point.

When the pandemic first ramped up, most weren't convinced that it would affect them or that they were going to get it. Some didn't think it was real, but most people were concerned. They wondered, will there be food shortages? Will there be power shortages? What's going to happen? Working mothers and fathers were particularly challenged because so much fell on them. And we've got to provide much better support for working parents.

Generally, there's a need for boundaries and parameters when working, whether in the office or at home. Just as you can't wear T-shirts with certain words on them at work, you shouldn't wear them on a Zoom call either. Attention must be paid to what's behind you or what image you might use as a virtual background.

You shouldn't have inappropriate photos, symbols, or other objects on display. There's always a need for boundaries and parameters in the workplace, regardless of whether the workplace is a building or a home office.

Most people want to be comfortable, and they want everyone else to be comfortable too. I think this more relaxed way of being will carry over as we transition back to work for most organizations. As we move back to more face-to-face interactions, we can expect to see more uncertainty about what should be worn and the new workplace rules. This is a golden opportunity for a hard restart of company and workplace culture. I think everyone realized this was a unique situation and tolerated a lot. For example, as much as people would like to control their dogs, babies, and noisy neighbors, we can't, and that's just the way it was. Thank goodness for the mute button—now, if only people would use it. We've all been in meetings in major cities prepandemic where fire trucks, ambulances, police cars, airplanes, and more could be heard. There's not much you can do to control that. There was a spirit of, we're all in this together, and people needed to be reasonable, patient, forgiving, and supportive.

It's hard to control the outbursts of a two-year-old, not to mention outbursts of people that are mature and much older. But I think most people show up at work every day wanting to do a good job. Many managers don't believe that, but most people show up at work trying to do good things and a good job. And the same is true of people working remotely. I generally give people the benefit of the doubt. People who don't want to do a good job rarely go to work, don't show up, call in sick, or do whatever they can to avoid work.

This pandemic has also forced organizations to become more agile. The leaders that could not let go were replaced or took the organization down with them. In many cases, they were forced to get the hell out of the way so more forward-thinking and agile managers could take over. Companies learned how to be agile quickly out of necessity and put people in charge of things because they had to. There was no time to tell people what to do, how to do it, or when to do it—it had to get done. The luxury of time was gone. They were forced to put people in charge, saying, "This is what we've got to do. Go figure it out, go do it. And you don't need to report back to me every hour, every day, every week—just do it. I don't have time to micromanage things; you just have to go."

I'm sure there are terrific offerings in agility and how to make an organization more agile, but at its core, it's really about trust, transparency, and empowerment. It's about letting people do the best job they can and giving them the resources they need. As long as people felt they had those resources, they could get the job done.

The lesson that was really driven home, in my observation, was that organizations are made up of people. It's all about people and how you treat them. Do you trust your people, nurture them, empower them? How you treat people is critical.

And in that vein of employee care and empowerment, leaders now need to be sensitive about their employees' well-being in new and different forms. Now that we are meeting and working remotely, there are new stresses and demands on our people. Working from home can be less stressful in many ways, but it can also be as bad as being in the office. As managers, we need to try to take care of the whole person. We need to be very sensitive to the stress that children, pets, houseguests, and other responsibilities create. This was unheard of just a short time ago.

Our world has been turned upside down, and a whole new type of stress has been thrust upon all of us. We've seen the unbelievable mental strain this has put on most of us. There were unprecedented levels of stress in the workforce as everything changed overnight and remained in flux for over a year in some cases. Leaders need to address these issues.

Forty-two percent of Americans reported symptoms of anxiety and depression in a survey taken in December of 2020, four times higher than the previous year. That's a four-fold increase in anxiety and depression. Deaths in the US from overdoses grew by 25 percent from August 2019 to August 2020. The toll this situation has taken on people for any number of reasons was dramatic. These increases and the need for mental health counseling forces organizations to think and operate differently.

Recently, there was an article by Deborah Schroeder-Saulnier in *Harvard Business Review.* She said, "Pandemic-related job and income losses have been much higher for women than men around the globe. As a business leader, you must act now to address this disparity and retain women in your organization, especially as you consider a return to office policies."[28] In my business and coaching practice, I talk to a number of women whose kids are now at home because the schools are closed. On top of that, they are running businesses and working remotely. Many people suddenly found themselves in a situation where they were the childcare provider for their family—usually, this was the woman. They were strapped with the stress of educating their kids, dealing with them when trying to work, and whatever else was happening at their home. It was overwhelming.

One particular friend is an entrepreneur, and her business was extremely busy during that time, and she had to take care of her school-aged child. I saw firsthand how difficult and stressful that situation was. She met the challenge like a hero, but what saved her and many others was that school eventually opened up, and she got back to some semblance of normalcy. Some people hired people to help them, but many couldn't. It was a huge problem.

Moving forward, we need to continue to empower our employees. Considerable empowerment took place; we must not let things slip back into the way they were. A lot of companies bought chairs, desks, or computers to help their employees be comfortable. That became common quickly. Managers were forced to listen and respond to people's needs. So, if they needed a better camera on their computer, they got one. If their internet

[28] Deborah Schroeder-Saulnier, "To Retain WOMEN, U.S. Companies Need Better Childcare Policies," *Harvard Business Review*, September 9, 2021, https://hbr.org/2021/05/to-retain-women-u-s-companies-need-better-childcare-policies.

connection was too slow, it was upgraded. In a sense, these work-at-home employees had a bit of the company under their control, so the company was forced to help them make it operational. Individuals also needed to become savvier about technology with this shift to an online world. Maximizing their video and sound quality, the speed of their connection, and other details they previously wouldn't have had to worry about suddenly became their responsibility.

Around the world, and in some large areas of the US, many people don't have an internet connection. There's not even the infrastructure for it. This was a challenge before COVID; now, it's become a critical issue. So many people were forced online to work or attend school from home, and many simply could not do it. Some didn't have the internet, while others didn't even own a computer. So much of the world is online now that a connection to the internet is almost a necessity. Coupled with the fact that many people had to stay at home, and many facilities, businesses, and services were shut down, they had very few options.

As painful as it may have been, many CEOs are glad they were forced to use tools like Slack or Chanty. They see the power of these tools and what they can do for them, but there is still an issue of access for many individuals.

The fallout from the pandemic is massive and almost incalculable. American Multi-Cinema (AMC), which runs many big movie theatres across the US, went from $450 million a month in revenue to less than $1 million a month. Think of all the people that AMC employed in one role or another. A multibillion-dollar business almost completely disappeared overnight. The CEO reported in *Fortune* magazine that he laid everybody off, including himself. AMC has since reopened, but many businesses will never reopen. Only companies with large hordes of cash were able to weather this event.

Several pieces of legislation provided for paycheck protection program loans through the CARES act. Other programs allowed companies to get low-interest loans from banks. People found ways to survive. Some large restaurants were forced to close but used their kitchens and money to provide food for people in need.

More data is coming from the fallout of the pandemic. Only time will tell what the real price tag is for the cost of the pandemic.

Many people were mad that they were getting laid off, but unfortunately, payroll is usually the largest expense a company has. There's usually no other option when trying to cut costs other than to reduce staff, furlough people, and eliminate positions. That's just a reality.

But even the companies that were surviving cut compensation back by 25 percent or more. Some companies boomed during the pandemic, and there was much conversation about modifying executive compensation in those companies that benefited from the pandemic. Many people looked at it like this. I may owe you a $200,000 bonus as CEO, but our business only grew so much because of the pandemic, and it wasn't anything you did as CEO. You just happened to be in the right place at the right time. There still is conversation among public and private companies about what should be done about this situation. It's a very difficult situation because many organizations had to make severe cuts in payroll, benefits, and allowances to mitigate the loss of business. There's just nothing an organization like AMC can do other than lay off people. It's terrible, but it's often better to lay off a portion of the workforce than to shut the whole business down because you weren't willing to make those hard decisions.

As you can imagine, it's tough to keep morale up during times like this. It calls for authenticity, transparency, and realizing this has a dramatic personal impact on people. You need to do whatever you can to support people.

In forty years of work, I've never been through a major layoff. I've been blessed to have worked for companies that had a great cash flow. I did work as a consultant in one organization where I had to lay off a newly hired group of people. The organization hired ten or twelve fairly senior people to form an internal consulting business. As an interim vice president, my boss, the CFO, didn't want to support this group anymore—he told me to get rid of those people. So, one Monday morning, I had to lay off twelve newly hired senior people. Some had moved across the country and relocated their families to take the job. It was absolutely the most gut-wrenching, terrible thing I've ever had to do in my career. It was devastating. I couldn't go back to work until the next day.

Some of them did find jobs in the organization, but honestly, I don't know what happened to all of them. It still bothers me. The most difficult thing was that since most were new to the organization, they got little severance. It's not uncommon if you've been in a company for a long time to get a severance when you get laid off, maybe one week of pay for every year you've worked at the company. But these people were all new, so they got little. I thought that was really crappy.

The supply chain took a huge hit, and it is still stumbling back online as of this writing. It's been fascinating from some viewpoints because it's caused many conversations to take place about controlling the supply chain better. We need more national stockpiles of protection equipment, food, water, and more. There were serious discussions about protectionism, moving some of the manufacturing moved offshore back to the US. Capitalism and democracy came to a head over some of these issues; there was a lot of finger-pointing. Most people couldn't have anticipated the amount of personal protective equipment needed by health care providers and a host of other organizations. There are now much larger inventories of products in people's hands than ever before.

This has also heated up the ongoing fight between sales and marketing people and the finance people. Most finance people hate inventory. They want to run as low on inventory as possible because sitting inventories are wasted money in their minds—stuff on shelves is money that is not gaining interest. I've been in many heated battles with finance people over inventory. But I think there's a whole new level of understanding now. Some of the finance people are seeing that inventory buffer is insurance to cash flow. The disruption was huge because so many companies had low inventory and they had to lay off people.

There were shortages in so many places, and heroic things were done, like countries and large organizations flying military aircraft to distribution centers and manufacturing plants worldwide to bring products in—versus the traditional channels of ocean freight transportation—to keep the supply chain going. President Trump sent military planes worldwide to get products out of plants that couldn't afford to wait for weeks as things went through customs, etc. Our current president has started a task force to look at some of these significant supply chain-related issues.

It's incredibly complicated. For example, it's affected so many areas that there's a huge shortage of cars right now due to the lack of computer chips. It's kind of a domino effect that devastated the supply chain. I am sure the entire supply chain will be reanalyzed and reworked to some degree. I don't know what's going to come out of all that. Still, it's caused virtually life-threatening situations for many providers who couldn't get technology, drugs, personal protection equipment, ventilators, and what they needed to take care of people.

As momentous as the supply chain crisis was, the damage to organizational culture was no less destructive. Crises reveal the real culture, and that was true in this case. It was very difficult to maintain a culture when they weren't able to operate face-to-face. As I mentioned earlier, it's all about the people. Organizations are made up of people, and leaders have to show they care. And, as I reported earlier, there are unprecedented levels of stress in the workforce that have to be addressed.

I do believe a new competitive landscape will emerge. Companies are flatter, faster, more agile, and customers have different needs and wants. McKinsey did a survey recently where they surveyed many leaders, and most said that the world will change, but only a few felt they were prepared for things to change drastically over the next five years. Very few actually felt prepared to address the coming challenges.

One thing good that's come out of all this is the reporting about the situation from so many angles. *The Wall Street Journal, Fortune, Forbes,* and more have been watching this closely and reporting anything people are doing to make the situation better. This has been very helpful for leaders because we've had to take lessons from so many different places and people.

One thing we have been forced to discover is that remote work benefits both management and employees. It was a quick and painful evolution to remote work, but we learned a lot. But dealing with the anxiety of returning to the office will be difficult for many people. Some have gotten comfortable not having to commute every day—getting on a bus, waiting for a cab, paying for an Uber, driving a car down a congested highway, or fighting for a seat on the train. It all seems like too much now that they've worked at home.

Managers will have to be flexible and realize that it will be very difficult to force people to do certain things now. Some leaders will try, but I think it will be an evolution of understanding what jobs need to be done face-to-face and which can be done remotely. A hybrid approach might work for some people. Going in only on certain days where face-to-face or other activities occur can be the balance people want. One thing we've learned is that working remotely is more cost-efficient. There are so many expenses cut out on both the employees' and the employers' sides when a person works remotely.

Accenture's global consulting firm has over 500,000 employees; many of those people have been working remotely for a long time. That's just the nature of their work. They seem to make it work. What can we learn from them?

No matter what we discuss, it always comes down to the customer. You have to take care of the customer above all else. I have spent my whole career in the health care, pharmaceutical, medical device space, and I think customer care will be one of the biggest challenges facing those industries. Customer needs and wants have changed, and no one knows exactly how to deal with those changes just yet. It's going to be very difficult for the average customer service salesperson to do the things they were doing prepandemic. I can only talk about my experiences in the US hospital business. Still, I don't think large companies with thousands of people employed in their workforce doing sales activity can maintain those organizations in the future. I think there will be significant cutbacks, and organizations will reduce the time that people can spend with a salesperson. There will be dramatic changes in how companies "go to market" around the world. It's going to be very difficult for these organizations to figure things out going forward.

It's going to be something that evolves over time, but salespeople, particularly in the medical device and pharmaceutical space, are very expensive. You can't just flip a switch and say everything's going digital. People don't have the bandwidth to deal with digital stuff. There's will have to be a hybrid approach. Some customers will want to go back to a face-to-face system, while others will want to do transactions digitally.

It's going to require a tailored approach which will be different for people worldwide.

*

The pandemic has changed the world in numerous ways, and its impact on business cannot be overstated. This event has touched almost every aspect of life, and the world will never be the same. The pandemic has had devastating effects on many people and organizations, but there has been a lot of good that came out of it as well. We need to embrace those changes and remain open to new and better ways of operating.

Our organizations have become much leaner; let's keep it that way. People are more empowered, and that's a great thing. Of course, some have lost a lot, even everything, and I don't mean to make light of that in any way. I am well aware of the pain and loss that has occurred; I just hope we will not let the good that has come out of this horrible situation go to waste.

APPENDIX

The leaders for whom I worked who had a positive impact on my development as a leader:

LEADER	ORGANIZATION
David Gammon	Stater Bros.
Ronald W. Burkle	Stater Bros.
David R. Pitts	Ochsner Foundation Hospital and Pitts Management Associates, Inc.
David R. Page	Ochsner Foundation Hospital
Dale L. Bankston	Metropolitan Hospital Council of New Orleans
Robert J. Baker	University Hospital Consortium
Richard M. Morehead	Abbott Laboratories
Sean E. Murphy	Abbott Laboratories
Christopher A. Kuebler	Abbott Laboratories
Josef Wendler (deceased)	Abbott Laboratories
Richard G. Ganz	Abbott Laboratories
Richard A. Gonzalez	Abbott Laboratories
Christopher B. Begley	Abbott Laboratories
Pierre Guyot	Mölnlycke Health Care
Andreas Joehle	Mölnlycke Health Care
Phillip M. Cooper	Mölnlycke Health Care
Graeme Brookes	Reapplix (via management contract)

Big Red's Personal Credo

Whomever you serve, serve them
with caring and respect.

Whatever you do, do it with passion and integrity.

Whenever you reach, reach beyond your grasp.

Wherever you go, go as a leader.

Above all, have fun.

ACKNOWLEDGEMENTS

STIFLED IS THE RESULT OF DISPARATE forces. My journey into the study of leadership took off at the B. Dalton bookstore in the Vernon Hills Mall in Illinois on May 20, 1990. I don't recall what precisely drove me to purchase *On Becoming a Leader* by Warren Bennis, but that decision started my passion for studying leadership.

I had wanted to write for some time but did not begin to pursue this hobby seriously until the end of 2014 when I started making notes for *Stifled*, following the completion of my eight-year run as president of the Americas at Mölnlycke Health Care. I had also begun to work on a memoir which I had been talking about writing for an embarrassingly long time and is still in process. Much of my writing efforts and energies since 2014 have been focused on the memoir. I have had amazing support for the memoir from many people and, most importantly and significantly, my wife, Nancy.

Her patience and encouragement with my episodic isolation as I buried myself in the memoir and attended writers' conferences and retreats and Zoomed with my writing groups are extraordinary and well beyond being a supportive spouse.

My sons, Marc and Matt, their spouses, and my new granddaughter, Hannah, have continued to inspire me throughout my life. Having children, their partners, and a grandchild are the greatest gifts of all.

A new and renewed inspiration to work on my writing and, in particular, the memoir, occurred when I took a year off to be part of the Inaugural Cohort of Stanford's Distinguished Careers Institute (DCI) in 2015. It was there I met John Evans, the instructor for English 91, Creative Nonfiction. John and seven marvelous, accepting, and patient Stanford undergrads allowed me to join their class; they embraced me throughout the semester. I finally dedicated time to writing and learning about the craft.

During the pandemic, I opened the file from *Stifled* and realized that if I didn't get some help with this, it would never get done. That's when I came across Leaders Press and agreed to work with them on this project.

I've been so fortunate over my forty-year career to have worked for some amazing managers. The list in the appendix does not do justice to this group. . .virtually everyone after my first manager, Dave Gammon, became an entrepreneurial success or a CEO or an officer in a major public or private company. I loved my time with those individuals.

For nearly twenty years, Paula Grimes has been at my side, tirelessly helping me manage my businesses. I could not have done what I have without her support and dedication.

I have thoroughly enjoyed my work with Leaders Press, primarily dealing with Grace O'Donnell and from time to time with Deborah Brannon. Luke Ahern helped me bring the subject to life. Grace has been a patient, calming force and a delight to work with, keeping me on track and focused. Thank you to the copyeditor, Wendy Hall.

One of my DCI Fellows from 2015, Kate Jerome, a seasoned publishing executive and award-winning children's book author, has been more than supportive whenever I needed her input, suggestions, and expertise. Thank you, Kate!

I was overjoyed to spend an afternoon with Warren Bennis in 2011, thanks to the help of two friends at the University of Southern California, Debbie MacInnis and Sarah Peyron Murphy. Warren was gracious and signed my copy of his book, *On Becoming a Leader*, with the inscription (in part), "This is my favorite book (of those he had written)."

I earned my executive MBA in 2009 from the Goizueta School at Emory and encountered an entire curriculum curated by fabulous professors and instructors, a few of whom have become dear friends and mentors. Charlie Goetz and Rick Gilkey, who were kind enough to write the foreword, are two of those. Rick understood my passion for leadership and mentored me during my time at Mölnlycke Health Care. I will always be deeply appreciative of his guidance and wisdom. Charlie was always gracious with his time, the greatest gift of all.

"It takes a village" is cliché but, for me, very true. Roughly midway through my eleven years at Abbott, then president of the Abbott International Division, Robert L. Parkinson, Jr., spoke to us in May 1996 on his ten principles of leadership. Most of his message was about people:

- "Our most important decisions made as managers are the people we hire.
- The concept of continuous improvement has its greatest potential with people, not machines.

- Be committed to developing people: most have more potential than ever realized but need a leader to nurture their confidence."

Bob became a dear friend after I left Abbott and when he retired from Abbott, both in 2000; he became a mentor, confidant, and cheerleader. He would always carve out time for me, and I relished the time we had together. The impact of a great leader like Bob goes way beyond those who reported directly to him and penetrates far outside the walls of an organization.

To those individuals I have had the distinct honor of leading, thank you in part for being the inspiration for *Stifled.*

ABOUT THE AUTHOR

HAVING LED TEAMS IN THREE CONTINENTS over more than 40 years and consulted with over 100 companies, Jim has seen great leaders who have thrived and ones that have flailed. A noted expert in leadership, Jim's leadership lessons are as highly sought after by today's business students as they are Baby Boomers. From 2006 to 2014, Jim built a team at Molnlycke Health Care that grew the revenue over 7 times and the EBITDA over 20 times creating over $1BN growth in enterprise value and taking the US business from number 5 to number 1 in the served market with an employee satisfaction index over 95%. Jim is passionate about diversity and inclusion and hosted a two day meeting for all women in the organization (not just high potentials) to discuss their unique challenges. Jim focuses now on coaching and mentorship and spreading his leadership lessons to help individuals become better leaders and organizations create great leaders.

https://jimwetrich.com/stifled-checklist